WITHIN THESE WALLS

WITHIN THESE WALLS

CONTROL

BY

ALAN MORRISON

iUniverse, Inc.
Bloomington

WITHIN THESE WALLS
Control

iUniverse books may be ordered through booksellers or by contacting:

iUniverse
1663 Liberty Drive
Bloomington, IN 47403
www.iuniverse.com
1-800-Authors (1-800-288-4677)

Because of the dynamic nature of the Internet, any web addresses or links contained in this book may have changed since publication and may no longer be valid. The views expressed in this work are solely those of the author and do not necessarily reflect the views of the publisher, and the publisher hereby disclaims any responsibility for them.

Any people depicted in stock imagery provided by Thinkstock are models, and such images are being used for illustrative purposes only.
Certain stock imagery © Thinkstock.

ISBN: 978-1-4620-5696-5 (sc)
ISBN: 978-1-4620-5698-9 (hc)
ISBN: 978-1-4620-5697-2 (ebk)

Printed in the United States of America

iUniverse rev. date: 10/11/2011

THE TRAVESTY OF MAN V'S

BOOK ONE   The Church
BOOK TWO   The State

THE FABLE AND DOWNFALL OF MAN

Psalms : 118.8

**"It is better to put your trust in the Lord
than put confidence in Man"**

(this is the exact center of the Bible)

BOOK ONE

The Church

PREFACE

The purpose of this book is to explain how people are brainwashed and controlled from childhood to adults, being "**controlled**" by the leaders of our society.

You must have an **open mind** when you read this book. We will present things that the church and state will not tell you and they do not want you to know.

We will explain that god's world is spirituality for his people and religion is man's idea of what he would like god's world to be for himself! How the church tries to convince us that religion and spirituality are the same. Religion and spirituality are 180 degrees apart. God is alive and well, but religion is the major question.

Many centuries ago when man started the cycle of civilization, a leader was required to keep things in order. As time went on, he also understood the necessity to thank someone for all the wonderful things that civilization had to offer. This created the god's to pray to. This is when the church and state were one.

At that time the control of the populace became very powerful by the powers to be, allowing the spoils of the people to go to one overseer, King or Pharaoh. But after many centuries, the ruler in power realized there was a problem with the system. That is when the church and the state separated, or did they? Now when something went wrong, the gods were getting blamed for getting angry, so the rulers did not lose their power. Instead of man gaining control of his life, now he was caught in the jaws of a vice. The church on one side saying what the gods wanted and the state on the other side saying what they wanted, caught in the jaws of evil. This was done so smoothly, that man never saw it coming. Then man was told that this is the way it is supposed to be to appease everybody.

So, now let's come up to today, where man is being brainwashed into thinking this is the way it should be. Everyone that is taken to church as a very small child, before that child is able to think for themselves, is been brainwashed by the church elders. There are many subjects that must be uncovered into reality to understand the message of this book.

There is one area about which most people are getting confused. There is no connection between religion and spirituality. Religion is mans idea of how he would like god's world to be for himself through **control** and brainwashing. That is why we have so many different religions in the world today, man's law of control. Spirituality, on the other hand, is the free will of each individual person, who answers only to himself and his god, without any input or influence from any outside source, just one faith throughout the world, only one universal god. Before the organized church got started, there was a group of people that believed you do not need a leader to have a church, only to believe in the higher power, "God". I would call these people true spiritualist. Once the church got started, due to the pressure from the church, this group slowly disappeared.

A short note about the writer of this book, I have been a workaholic all my life. I do not remember ever sitting down to read a book or taking the time to sit down to write anything, even a letter. Recently, I had some spare time, and my god told me to sit down and start writing. The following is what I was told to write. After finishing this writing, I had to go back and read what was written, saying to myself, I wrote this? This is when I realized that this message was not meant for me alone, but for everybody to read. Please read—Psalms 118:8—"It is better to trust in the Lord than to put confidence in man". (Center of Bible).

There is nothing in this book that will take away from a belief or understanding of who god is, only the church and what it stands for. Religion is not what the church tries to tell you or explain to you!

Here is a list of subjects that must be uncovered and investigated into reality for today's lifestyle and truth. What the church (religion) does not want you to know.

Chapter one;   The Bible
Chapter two;   The Old Testament
Chapter three;   Muslim and the Koran
Chapter four;   The Church
Chapter five;   Religion
Chapter six;   God
Chapter seven;   Intuition
Chapter eight;   Prayer
Chapter nine;   Pastor / Minister / Rabbi and etc.
Chapter ten;   Spirituality
Chapter eleven;   Jesus and U F O's
Chapter twelve;   Christmas and Easter
Chapter thirteen;   Reincarnation
Chapter fourteen;   The Devil and Lucifer
Chapter fifteen;   Exorcism
Chapter sixteen;   Bible Bashers and Do Gooders
Chapter seventeen; Astrology

INTRODUCTION

Starting with the Bible, Theologians and Scholars will agree that it is the most FANTASTIC STORY BOOK ever written. What they won't tell you is how incomplete it is, that it is almost worthless. The majority of the scriptures were not included by man because he thought he would lose too much control of the masses if these messages were included. Secondly, the bible is not the word of god. It is the message of god, as interpreted by man, as understood by man, as translated by man (the church elders). So now what do we have? Good question. Example—tell one person a fact, and then pass it around to ten people, what comes out at the end is nothing like it started. In view of these translations, where does that leave the most published book in the world? Most people are brainwashed into believing the bible is unequivocally the word of god. This is the furthest thing from the truth. The reason the stories in the bible do not say anything specific, is so the High Priest may interject his interpretation to maintain control of the populace based on the situation at that time. We are back to the first objective, maintaining control of all the followers. If all the original scriptures were included in the bible, there would be so much controversy and contradiction, the Priest would have lost control way before the Old Testament was ever created, enough for now.

The church, if you believe anything In the bible, Jesus said a church is a gathering of three or more people. Where in any writing does it say, build me the grandest and most elaborate building or cathedral in honor of me? The bible says to tithe. Then there was the church rendition (ten percent) to maintain control so the high priest can live the life of luxury. How can the church which is supposed to be a faith, own a state or country, The Vatican? By control of the masses, this should never have been allowed to happen. How can pedophiles and murderers be protected by the church? This contradicts any church doctrine. But it goes on every day, "**control**". The church has more blind power over the people than most people realize. The bible says do not lie, but it is promoted constantly by the church. Read between the lines, the church says, come confess your sins, so you can be forgiven, then go do it again to be forgiven again and again by man, not god. If the church is of, and for god, why do we have so many different denominations? The reason is so simple, just take a good look at it. Each individual sect has its own rules and guidelines set down by man. He says (man), I don't like the way you control your people, so I will start a new division under my ideas (man's control), such as what is this nonsense to pray five times a day facing east, (Muslim) control?

✠

What is religion? Religion is the biggest travesty of all. It is a division of the state under the guise of god. What, you say you know it is not true? If not, why are there so many laws and rules by the state specifying how a religious sect must do business? The only freedom a "recognized" religion has is if they follow the rules of the state first. They do not pay taxes. The same as any other department of the state, who else does not pay taxes?

Religion has been passed down over the centuries by a continuous brainwashing, being told that this is what is best for man. So many people have to go to church every week religiously, because they are brainwashed into this habit or do not understand the doctrine of the Church or realize what has taken place. Religion, is a word or belief of what you have been taught since childhood? Religion is nothing more than a following as prescribed by the teachings of man. Religion has become a very acceptable way to hold the populace in check.

Come hear our song, it makes you feel good, listen to me try to interpret the good book and collect your money. There is nobody that can interpret the Bible for anybody else. It is written in such a manner that only you can get the proper understanding only to yourselves, not from any person or any another source. Anybody that says they can interpret the good book for you is only propagating the brainwashing.

✠

God, now this is the question of all ages. Who or what is god? The only people who have the true answer are the Native American Indians that I have any knowledge of. How can one being or entity be omniscient, at all times, and omnipresent? The American Indians, I believe are the only people of ancient times that never lost sight of who they are, where they came from, and who god is.

Each and every person in our universe is a unique individual. Therefore everybody has their own individual god. The Indians look to their elders, present and deceased for guidance and knowledge. When a person dies, their physical body is, in all rights, waste material. But their spirit or soul moves on to the next plain. Our ancestors or spirits of loved ones are with us at all times. If, as Jesus said, three people make a church, therefore three or more spirits create a church for that person which is that persons god.

✠

Intuition, many times is most often referred to as woman's intuition, it is the freedom of the mind to hear your god speaking to you. Referred to as a woman's trait, because they hear god speaking to them more often where usually men will want to rationalize the situation first. Your first instinct is something very few people understand. This is almost always the word or information from your god and is almost always the right answer. Most males are so used to trying to rationalize the situation based on their training, they overlook the obvious, taking minutes to days looking for the best results, when they usually end up with their first instinct in the end.

✠

Prayer is something most people understand only to a small degree. The church tells you that this is something you should do everyday without defining how or what the purpose of a prayer is. A prayer is an extension of your emotions that comes from your heart, not for something that you want as personal gain.

A prayer vigil is when many people get together for prayer. This in turn gets many spirits together to provide help for the person being prayed for, THE POWER OF GOD. The power of god is when the individual gods come together for a common purpose and the greater the mass of gods, the stronger the prayer is for the person being prayed for.

What is the purpose of prayer? Prayer has become a method for people to appease themself. The average person will sit down and confess to god (themselves) about all the things they have done wrong, and ask forgiveness from themself. The average person knew when they did something wrong, it was not right, but also, say I will confess my sins and be forgiven. Lying to someone is bad, but lying to yourself is unforgivable. There are situations where asking for help for someone else is a wonderful thing, but if this prayer is not truly from the heart, it is a waste of time and effort. Only a few times, when a prayer vigil is truly effective, is when the people praying are truly honest. Sometimes when a prayer vigil is happening, the Participants are there only for show. It makes them feel good about themselves. I myself cannot remember sitting down just to pray. I want to live my life as a prayer, so I do not have to ask for forgiveness for something I have done. When I do ask for help in a prayer, I do not bow my head in shame or fold my hands in rejection. I lift my head high, proud, to the heaven where my god is. I turn my hands, palm up to receive the energy of the universe. That is the same as many cover their head with a shawl or other article of cloth in a so called religious service. Covering the head is rejecting god's power and the energy of the universe. This tradition was created by man to keep the masses under control.

✝

Ministers, Pastors, Rabbi's, etc, these are men of god. Bull. These men have good intentions, but very far from the truth. They go to school (brainwashed by man's school) to learn how to control the masses. How to interpret the bible so man will think he is on the right track. They will read the scriptures and interpret them to what is necessary at the time. Give ten theologians the same passage and you will get ten versions of what it means. As I said earlier, the bible, as used today is a farce. The bible is a storybook only to be used to control the masses. All "Men of God" that I have met will say the same thing. But what they don't realize is they are the most brainwashed of all (for power). They believe what they are doing is good for the people, when in reality, these men are actually a government official. You ask how can I say such a thing? Well it's like this, the church governing bodies, from Theology school down to the alter boys must follow the laws of the state, before they can follow the rules of the church (man's rules). Again, control, hidden control.

While on this subject, can anybody tell me how being a "Man of the Cloth" has become a profession? This profession was started so far back in time when all the gods were in power that we are brainwashed into believing that this a legitimate profession. Being a man of the cloth should be by **faith** to expand god's word, not just a way of life to provide a living. We have been so brainwashed into believing that this practice is necessary by the church that it is hard to imagine life any other way.

✝

With respect to spirituality, the only true nation that is spiritual that I know of is the American Indian's. The largest travesty is when these people were forced also to include Christianity into their lifestyle. As long as these people maintain the spirituality of their elders, they will survive the curse and control of man. These people have done a wonderful job so far, as long as Christianity never gets any stronger in their society, fantastic. If the present elder's had a method to get Christianity out of their life, they would maintain a true level of spirituality.

There are many spiritualists in the world today, but society frowns on them. There are many forms of spirituality. Because the average person does not understand what spirituality is (due to their brainwashing from the church), this leaves a big hole for **fakes** to appear and capitalize on the situation. There are so many people that believe in god, and know that there is something else out there, but do not have the guidelines to show them the right way to reach it. This is how **fakes** can get into the mainstream and ruin the only true "Religion" which is **spirituality**. Spirituality answers only to itself and its own god, nobody else, no person, or false god. Now guess what? If spirituality were to become much stronger, the state and church would no longer have total control over the masses. As the more people that would turn to spirituality, the church of today will crumble, leaving the state in shambles. The more the state would shatter, the less departments the state needs, the less taxes they need, and the more the state can equalize living conditions for its now free people. The more this takes place, the smaller the state government body becomes, the fewer freeloaders that can be found, Welfare—all but gone. Unemployment compensation—all but gone. With man on a free role, you'll see a massive explosion of New Technology to surpass the twentieth century by leaps and bounds.

☩

Jesus and U F O's. Let's start with UFOs. These crafts and their Inhabitants have been around earth since the oldest record of man. The oldest recorded (by man) history is the caveman. Caveman drawings very clearly show "flying saucers" in many of their cave drawings. If there are these records that far back, what is wrong with the State, that our government is continually saying that they don't exist? Do the ones in power think that the populace is that stupid? Ancient times had drawings carved in buildings and paintings depicting UFOs. If you look at a specific Era of time when UFOs appear the most prevalent for a time period, then look at the time line of Jesus. There are so many pictures being uncovered that definitely have a saucer in the picture. And the state still denies their existence today. Now let's put the fact straight. Our neighbors, the alien's have a pact not to interfere with the progress of the human race. So let's face the facts into reality. Mary had a son called Jesus, half human, half another race? When he was born, three wise men saw a light and followed it to honor the new King. The light in the sky that they followed was not a star. That does not follow any reasoning of physics for a star to shine like a spotlight so bright to announce the birth of a human child. It does follow suit that Jesus other half race, did shine a light to announce the birth of one of their own from their spacecraft. This type of a light has been seen in recent years and known to come from a UFO. For the best understanding I have, I believe that there is more than one alien race watching us. Based on my personal experience of encounters with UFOs, back in 1984, in Tucson Arizona watching TV one evening, my wife and I heard a glass figurine break in the other room. Getting up to see what happen, what we discovered was amazing. Looking out of our kitchen window was a very large UFO, with red, blue, green, and white lights, hovering about 10ft. off the ground. Once we acknowledge their presence, they left, but what they left behind was the most astonishing thing. We had a plant on the kitchen counter that was a ball of full bloom flowers. When the UFO left, the plant leaned completely toward where the craft was. We immediately called the Ufologist in Tucson, AZ, who came to our house that night. After hours of making the report, the plant was taken to the University of Arizona. Within three days we got a call, asking what kind of soil and fertilizer were used. We told them the commercial brand. These calls went on for two years. After two years of testing, the University of Arizona came back stating that they had no idea what happened to or what was in the soil or plant. They could not identify the chemical composition to anything known on earth at that time. That same evening, every plants in the backyard did the same thing; they all leaned at forty five to seventy degrees toward the direction where the UFO was. The next morning, in the daylight, there was a very large pattern, perfect circle in the soil of an empty field where the craft had landed for about twenty minutes. Is this the same thing that happens when crop circles appear?

✝

Astrology. This is the most confusing subject that I have encountered. There seems to be a major contradiction from what history tells us and what today's religion is telling us. The Ancient Egyptians, Greeks, Persians, and Romans had their god's to pray to. When you go back and study the life of their gods, you will find out that today's religion seems to have originated completely on the god's of Pagan times. You will discover that the rituals of today's church are the same as what was practiced way back in Pagan times.

CHAPTER ONE

The Bible

According to Webster's dictionary, the bible is considered to be the authority of the Christian religion, please note the wording, considered. There is nothing saying this is the authority positive. Much of the bible, if written today would be a simple story of someone's life. According to the bible, Christianity started at the time of Jesus Christ. Now if this is true, where did the Old Testament come from? The Old Testament came from the Jews and how old are the writings? The Jewish faith does not recognize Jesus as our savior. So if we recognize the Bible as the basis of Christianity, what is the Old Testament doing in there? This seems as a contradiction of itself? The church elders included the Old Testament to continue the Control of the masses. Everybody today accepts the bible as the source of Christianity, Jesus Christ, our lord and savior. There is nothing that different from most of scriptures of the bible, other then when it was written, that's different from somebody's family life of today. How can the Old Testament be the founding of Christianity when Jesus had not been born yet? The founding faith of the Jews rejected Jesus enough to kill him. The Roman's had Jesus killed to protect their faith and power over the masses. This was a time of turmoil for the state and church. That's when the Roman's told the Church to handle the situation. Then the church told the people that they had to decide the fate of Jesus. If this sounds a little far fetched, then go back and read the scriptures again. But as you do, read between the lines, and I hope you will see how the good book has an iron hold on your ability not to read between the lines and allow the church to control you. You will discover that the Old Testament was included so the church could maintain control of the masses.

This book, endorsed by the church has been the major factor in the church controlling its people. This is greatest storybook ever written. There are two major problems with this book. Most of the stories in the bible are every day occurrences of every day people. Because of the difference of the time period, and the translation, these stories sound so reverend. If I were to go out today and transcribe the every day happenings of many families, wouldn't I have myself a modern bible? If the bible was more inspirational than controlling, why are there so many books of scriptures not included in today's bible? When the church was putting the bible together, they were very cautious not to include anything that would affect their control. And the bible has been interpreted so many times and translated so many times, that there is no way that we can be sure that we are receiving the original intended message, if there was an intended message. Or was the original message that simple. This is the way our people conducted their lives. This is an example of how you should conduct your life. Can you tell me why in the bible, so many stories, of how people lived, became such a revered book? The church saw the opportunity, and these scriptures were written as a golden opportunity to use the life of Jesus as a controlling factor, to keep the masses in check. Please don't read something into these statements that is not there. I do not condone the complete bible. There are some very good stories of Jesus and why he was sent to us. Jesus came at a troubling time in the history of mankind. If we were able to remove from the bible, all the rhetoric nonsense that had nothing to do with Jesus, or why he was sent to us, then we might have a bible that made more sense. In simple words "KISS", "Keep It Simple Stupid". The more complicated, the more confusing, the easier it is to control the masses.

Now to continue with this ridiculous book, if the bible was such a great book as first translated and assembled, why isn't there just one bible? First you have the Catholic version, then you have many Protestant versions, and etc. Then you have many faiths that forbid their congregation to read certain versus or scriptures. Now, how is that for very obvious control? Then you have the Mormon book and the Amish, the Pennsylvania Dutch, Mennonites, and the Koran. This is before we go to Europe, Asia, and Africa. If we are all reaching for the same god, how can we all have a different set of rules? Everybody I know of would like to see world peace. So what is it going to take to get man's pride and ego out of all these faiths and religions, so we can have a common goal for mankind? Stop the fighting and killing in the name of religion. What we need to do, first of all, is get a coalition of many faith leaders to remove man's ego and pride out of the good book. Let's come to a common ground from a translation to print, about why Jesus came to us and what his life was meant to represent for all of us.

Let's get something straight. There many races on earth. There are many different colors, features, and sizes, but we all have only one god. As I said, of all of the races and cultures, let's get rid of individual pride and ego so we can become a more civilized world, not an animalistic society. This is what we are right now, animalistic in nature. We kill each other for what, national pride, and personal ego or in the name of religion? This makes us unintelligent and ignorant. No better than the animals that live in the wild. All you need to do is look at **Star Wars, Star Trek**, and all of the science fiction programs on TV. Do you believe that these writers, all use their imagination, or did their god's give them some insight of what is really out there? We have not progressed to this level yet. This is why we have UFOs that will not make contact with us. We are too much of an animal nature. We need to progress to the level we profess, but have not reached yet. As I said, back in the beginning, we need to get rid of the bible as we know it today. All of the present day scriptures and all the faiths around the world need to be combined and rewritten, or in other words, let's start from scratch and write a book of faith for all people so we can have one faith for the whole world. Then we can start acting like responsible humans and not animals. We are not a dumb people, but we are brainwashed into acting this way. This practice has to stop, so we, as a mass of people, can be free to think and advance as a universal power. To stop being concerned about being a world power and start thinking about how to become a friendly universal power. As long as we act like animals, killing each other for the sport of it, for pride, ego, profit, or in the name of religion, we are locking ourselves into a stagnant existence. This is what the Jewish nation and faith have done to themselves, fighting with their neighbors over land and a difference of faith. The stories in the Old Testament are almost childish. The Jewish faith does not recognize the New Testament. They are still fighting for the same land they were fighting for more than 2,000 years. When are you going to grow up and quit being so childish? No land, no war is worth fighting for in the name of religion or profit. The only war worth fighting is for the survival of the Human race. Like the movie "Independence day". This movie depicts our world coming together to fight off an alien attack on the Earth.

The bible is not the only big lie. Of all the religions that have their own good book, if these books were the word of god, how can there be so many variations from one book to the next. Every religion starts with a child (before being brainwashed), and continues on to the end with God. The beginning and end are the same. There are so many variations of the bibles, of each religion, that there have been wars fought over religion. Now let's look and read much closer to reality. The good book of each religion was written by man—THE STATE—so they could control the masses. If god or Jesus had anything to do with the writing of the bible, which controls every religion, they would read very much the same, with no need to fight over who is right or wrong. When the Bible and the Koran (or any other name) becomes a piece of trash, to get the state out of the church, we might begin to have peace in this world. The bible of each religion has been, and always will be the cause of wars until man realizes the destructive power of each and every bible around the world. Destroy all The Bibles and Koran to free man from control by the state.

I guess I need to explain a little about my statements, that the bible is a worthless storybook. What the true meaning of that statement is not really simple, but here goes. The Bible and Koran were written about 2,000 years ago. Many of the stories have lost their original meaning, they are obsolete. The lifestyle has changed drastically and the language has also changed drastically. I have met many people who try to read and understand the bible with no avail. So they have to go out and get a study bible. Now the problem is more complicated. There are so many different study bibles, which one to choose? This creates the same problem as the bible itself. Study bibles are again an interpretation of the original. Which one of these books has the most accurate interpretation? As I said earlier, nobody can give you an interpretation but yourself.

Something that the average person is not aware of is that most of the scriptures were not written at the time that they happened. Most of the scriptures were written about fifty to three hundred years after the fact. That means that these stories were passed down, translated how many times, before they were put on paper? So, as I said, how accurate is this great story book? The same as the Scriptures of Peter, Thomas, Judas, and Mary (Disciples) that was not included in the bible. Many of the scholars of today know that the bible is very incomplete, based on all of the information that is being uncovered by today's archeologist.

What we need is an intelligent group of people that will rewrite the bible to an understandable writing with the true meaning of the bible. Not a book that cannot be read or understood and every interpretation varies.

Now let's get into the true travesty of the bible. The original bible was not created by the Christian Church. The original bible was assembled by the Roman's around the third century. At that time, the leader of the Roman's thought that the Christian's had a great thing going. So the Pharaoh banned all of the Pagan Gods, and assembled the first bible, eliminating all the scriptures that he thought were not worthy to be included or did not maintain his control. All of the banned scriptures were then set aside. The Christians years later, picked up the bible as their own. Then they started to modify the bible to suit the church's (Priest's) doctrine and control. When they finished their changes, the remaining scriptures were discarded. There are only four original scriptures (The decuples,

Mathew, Mark, Luke, and John) in the bible. When the remaining scriptures were discarded, somebody took them, and sealed them in a large jar, and buried the jar which remained hidden for almost two centuries. As you can now see, do you still believe that the greatest, most published book in the world is a true Christian work of art? Or is the bible the greatest travesty ever presented to mankind? The bible is in all of time, according to this, the foundation of Christianity, is nothing more than the most controlling item that we have today. A storybook, so the church can control their populous? In simple words, the Christian Bible was not written or started at the time of Jesus, it only came into being after the Romans started what they thought was a good thing the people had working for them but actually gave the rulers more power. Another fact about the book is it is written that the world is Six thousand years old, which we know today as a fact that the world is much older than this.

SUMMATION

There are a few facts about the bible that most people do not know, that the Church does not want you to know. First, who assembled the first bible? It was not the Christians, it was the Romans. It is a fact that the Romans assembled the first bible for control. It only had four scriptures at that time. Second, almost none of the scriptures were written by who they are named for. Third, since the scriptures were written from stories, handed down, how many changes were made in the stories before they were written? Fourth, why were so many scriptures not included when the Christians assembled their version of the bible, control? I hope that you can now see what the message is. Do your own research if you feel that anything here is questionable. But wake up people, stop the brainwashing the church is doing to our children, stop the control. Finally, I believe 100% in god, but not in religion as it is today. If you take a good look at the church, you will discover that this is the largest Organized Crime in the world today. I am a spiritualist. A spiritualist believes in god and the power of the universe, not in religion

For some backup info, on the History Channel, aired on Dec. 25, 2004, a program titled "Banned from the Bible", Decoding the Past. May 24, 2007. Also, "Strange Rituals" aired on Nov. 14, 2009 and UFO'S in the Bible June 11 2005. On the Science Channel on Dec. 14, 2008 a program called "Exodus" and also "Sodom and Gomorrah" on April 6, 2009 "Lost Gospels"

CHAPTER TWO

THE OLD TESTAMENT

As I said earlier, the Old Testament should not be included in the bible that we use today. The main reason for this statement is very simple. Most of these stories are fiction. All of these stories were created before the time of Jesus and Christianity. Therefore, how can these scriptures be part of our Christianity or Moslem faith today? There are a few of the stories that have some validly, but the majority of them do not. Many of the stories were created by the church elders to keep the people in control. When the bible was being assembled, the church elders included the Old Testament in an effort not to lose control. The main problem with the Old Testament is that too many people take these scriptures as gospel, the word of god. This is very far from the truth. Let's take a look at the first chapter, Genesis. If Adam and Eve were the first people on earth, and they were Caucasian. Will somebody explain about all the other people on the earth? We have White, yellow, red, brown, and black skinned humans with us. If this story is accurate, where did these people come from? The Asians, Indians, Negros, and other races did not come from mid air. You cannot say they were cross bred since there was only one race to start with. Next, let's take a look at Noah and the Arc. Yes, there was a great flood that took place, but it was more localized than the story depicts. Since there was not any world wide communication at that time, the story was expanded into a great flood that covered the whole Earth. Example, the Mediterranean Sea, it has been proven that there was a great

Tsunami in ancient times that flooded the complete area around the Mediterranean Sea which thru stories passed down got changed into a great flood covering the whole earth, couldn't this account for the story being misconstrued to what it ended up being written? Again, I say, since there was only one couple on the Arc, which was Caucasian. Where did all the rest of the races come from? Did they just materialize out of thin air? Something else that needs explained, how did all the animals from each continent get to the arc and how did they all get back to their respective continent? The story of Sodom and Gomorrah has also been proven to be not accurate. Archaeologist have proven that there was a Meteor that came down to destroy the two cities. With a little common sense, you will see that these stories are just that, stories to keep the people under the control of the church. All of this took place at a time before the average person was very educated. People, we have been brainwashed for so long. It's time we start using our brain and looking thru what Organized Religion (Organized Crime) has been cramming down our throats.

SUMMATION

Since the Old Testament was written before Jesus came to earth, who contrived these stories? Some of the stories are true, some are stories of how people lived, and others were dreamed up by the powers to be for control. Many of these stories were dreamed up when the Romans had all of their gods to prey to. Many of the stories were written from stories passed down verbally and how they were changed over time thru translation, Therefore still maintaining full control of the masses.

CHAPTER THREE

MUSLIM AND THE KORAN

Since Christianity and the Muslim faiths make up the majority of religions in the world, here is something to think about. The Muslim Faith and the Koran are very similar to Christianity and the Bible. The Koran was written by only one man (supposedly), Mohamed, the prophet. The Muslim faith differs in the area, that they do not have the same organized church. Muslim has one god as the Christians do. Muslims believe that each person must answer to god themselves. There is so much similarity between the two faiths. The major difference is only in the semantics and interpretation of the bible and the Koran. The passages of the Koran have as much variation in interpretation as the bible. The Koran believes that only god can interpret these passages correctly. Now if this is the case, the Muslim people are under the same control as the Christian people. Except how we do our worshiping? As I explained earlier, everybody in the world is so brainwashed from child birth to death, it makes it very hard to see the truth of what our god wants for us. Repeating myself, each of us has our own god, no matter what faith you want to associate with. Mohamed set down rules as he understood them, the Christians have the Ten Commandments. These rules are very similar. It is a crying shame, all the fighting over semantics that the two books have put forth to the people of the world. The brainwashing that the Muslim faith has is so strong, if not stronger than any other faith. This creates a hidden control that is out of control. We have to stop brainwashing our children before they can think for themselves. The Muslim's are brainwashed so severally, that they will commit suicide for their religion. Does this sound like a rational persons thinking? We all need to listen to our own god, to become a better person in god's eyes. We must all stop listening to the elders or leaders of our faith, and listen only to our own god.

The populous that follows the Koran needs to start listening to their god only and stop following their Iman as the Koran says. The Koran says to answer to god only, not to what man is teaching. If the Muslim people will start following their own Koran which says that each person is to listen to their "GOD" and nobody else, they will discover that their Iman is not following what their good book states. The brainwashing in this religion is so strong and so far out of text that most of these people do not understand what their own Koran tells them to do! Stop listening to your Iman and start reading your good book so you can understand what it is telling you to do!

Something for the Muslim people to be aware of; the Koran has been modified and changed since it was originally written by Mohamed. The same as the bible has been changed. These changes have been made so the leaders can maintain control by both books.

I recently received an E-mail that must be shared. Since we are talking about control and brainwashing, this is the ultimate as follows which many Muslims do not fully understand.

* * *

"REMINDER OF THE BASIC BELIEFS OF ISLAM"

This is a true story and the author, Rick Mathes, is a well known leader in prison ministry. The man that walks with God always gets to his destination. If you have a PULSE you have a PURPOSE.

The Muslim religion is the fastest growing religion per capita in the United States, especially in the minority races!!!

Last month I attended my annual training session that is required for maintaining my state prison security clearance. During the training session there was a presentation by three speakers representing the Roman Catholic, Protestant, and Muslim faiths, who explained each of their beliefs.

I was particularly interested in what the Islamic Iman had to say. The Iman gave a great presentation of the basics of Islam, complete with a video. After the presentation, time was provided for questions and answers.

When it was my turn, I directed my question to the Iman and asked: "Please correct me if I'm wrong, but I understand that most Imans and clerics of Islam have declared a holy jihad (Holy War) against the infidel, (which is a command to all Muslims) they are assured of a place in heaven. If that's the case, can you give me the definition of an infidel?"

There was no disagreement with my statements and, without hesitation, he replied, "non-believers!"

I responded, "So, let me make sure I have this straight. All followers of Allah have been commended to kill everyone who is not of your faith so they can have a place in heaven. Is that correct?"

The expression on his face changed from one of authority and command to that of a little boy who had just been caught with his hand in the cookie jar. He sheepishly replied, "YES"

I then stated, "Well, sir, I have a problem trying to imagine Pope Benedict commanding all Catholics to kill those of your faith or Dr. Charles Stanley ordering all Protestants to do the same in order to guarantee you a place in heaven!"

The Iman was speechless!

I continued, "I also have a problem with being your friend when you and your brother clerics are telling your followers to kill me!"

Let me ask you a question: "Would you rather have your Allah, who tells you to kill me in order to go to heaven, or my Jesus who tells me to love you because I am going to heaven and He wants you to be there with me?"

You could hear a pin drop as the Iman hung his head in shame. Needless to say, the organizers and/or promoters of the

"Diversification" training seminar were NOT happy with my way of dealing with the Islamic Iman, and exposing the truth about the Muslim' beliefs.

In twenty years there will be enough Muslim voters in the U.S. to elect the President! (THEY did this very thing in November-2008)

I think every one in the U.S. should be required to read this, along with the ACLU; there is no way this will be widely publicized, unless EACH OF US sends it on!

*   *   *

Now we are talking about brainwashing and control. The above gives you an example of what is happening in our world today. This is not god's way; it is not what Allah originally wanted. THIS IS WHAT MAN HAS CREATED FOR HIMSELF. I have never heard of a god that wanted his people to kill anybody!! God only wants your sole, not your body. THIS IS BRAINWASHING AND CONTROL BY MAN!!

CHAPTER FOUR

THE CHURCH

The church as described by Jesus is a gathering of three or more people, not the "BUILDING". The building became the symbol of the church way back to the time of the Pharaohs, when they built temples and statues to every god that they had. How can the masses of today worship this false god, the building? I find many people today that do not feel they are going to church if they do not go to the fancy building to worship. Jesus said, do not worship false gods, But most religions today warship this false god. And there are so many chapels, temples, cathedrals, synagogues, and so on. All of these fancy and elaborate buildings are the idea only of the past, the ancient governments. The masses are duped into believing you cannot have a church without the fancy expensive building. So let's go back to when the fancy synagogues and cathedrals were built. Since the first chapels were built when the state and church were one, why does today's church continue with this practice? It's called brainwashing. These buildings are one of the church's largest holds on their masses because it makes people feel good when they go there. The bible says to tithe without any specified amount, which only means to support the church, but the church says to give ten percent of all you earn. Since god is non material, what good is all that money except to prosper the priests or minister? This ten percent has nothing to do with god's world, only man's. WAKE UP PEOPLE.

Now let's go inside the building, you have an altar. The start of the altar was in pagan times. This altar was used for sacrifice at that time. Our god wants your soul, not to sacrifice anybody or anything. So what is it doing in god's church? The altar today is a show of strength by the church. This is the first step to brainwashing the masses. The church today makes a beautiful scene of the altar, not for sacrifice, but to make you feel comfortable. I call this sideways brainwashing. Sideways brainwashing is when, in every day life, you see things that reinforce what you have been taught (brainwashed). Such as when you go down the street, and see a Cross, the Church building, or something else that refers to religion.

The church is not a fashion parade. Why is it deemed that everybody must wear their finest threads on Sunday? The people of these organizations have been brainwashed into believing that god grades us on appearance. Man has made the church a place of status and appearance. If you go to church on Sunday, in your dirty work clothes, you will be frowned upon. This control is by the state for financial gain. This again is a way of control by the state—OH—sorry the church. The average church does not allow children into normal church service. All children must first attend what is called "Sunday School". When man decides the children have been brainwashed enough, then they may attend regular Sunday services. First the church says what is right or wrong, and then reads the bible until the children have it planted in their head, that this is the only way. Now you can go upstairs into the chapel. Then the first thing you see is a crucifix or a cross. You are told this is what it is all about. The crucifix is a symbol of Jesus on the cross. Jesus said not to worship an idol, then what is the crucifix, if it is not an idol? The masses go to church to honor their god, who they don't know or understand, or have never seen, but they go to pay respect to an idle of the son, Jesus. This seems very confusing.

Next item of interest is the church, a nonprofit organization. This is one of the state's biggest lies. If the church is nonprofit, the building, in most situations, is one of the most expensive structures for its size. Many pastors and officials of the church drive better and newer vehicles than many of their followers. And the money spent on the church's Theologian schools is enormous. This is the opposite of nonprofit. But since the church is part of the state, this is OK. The church of today is not nonprofit. If you ask any church or government official, what part of one is part of the other, you will get a very positive denial. That's not unexpected. This has been going on for so many centuries, that nobody today recognizes the truth. Although neither body has any direct connection, it is very hard to find any connection at all. But the fact is that the church and state are the only two controlling factors that have 100% control over the masses of people. This means, if you don't get it from the left, you get it from the right. People, wake up and take control of your own life. Do not let the higher powers (church and state) maintain control of us. To fully understand what I mean, I hope you will understand a little more as you read on in this book.

Please take a deep look into this society. At this time in civilization, I cannot tell the difference between Organized Crime and Organized Religion. The Catholic faith is in shambles. How can a faith "OWN A COUNTRY" (the Vatican)? When a faith, the church collects so much money that they do not know how to spend it, that they buy priceless Jewels, Paintings, and other material objects, such as land, housing, and a Country in the name of GOD? When the church doctrine says to help the needy and poor, why are they spending it on material item and not helping the needy. Is this the same as the Mafia? Why has the Catholic Church never put out a financial statement? Is it because they have so much excess money that they do not want the general public to know how much they are worth? On the HINT channel a program aired on Dec 22, 2010 Secrets of the Vatican. They explain that the Italian Government gave the Catholic Church the land the Vatican is on. That the Jewels and artifacts are actually owned by the Italian people. If this is the truth, why aren't they in an Italian Museum?

It has been known for a long time that the church has been a wonderful place to hide, for child molesters, pedophile and sexual acts. For many years the church would move their priest from one location to another when it learned of a problem of sexual acts with children and/or adults of that particular parish. Isn't this the same as organized crime and a prostitution ring? Why does the Catholic Church not allow a priest or nun to marry outside of the church?

This allows the members of the church to act as a cult, to have free sex within the church organization? This practice goes back to the time of the Pharaohs. Doesn't this go against the moral rules of the church? Why does the priest chastise its members for having free sex with anyone, when it is a standard practice for the priests and nuns? This practice has been such a standard practice within the church, until recently, when it got so out of control, that there were many court cases that the church lost. This cost the church (organized crime) millions of dollars that should have gone to the poor and needy. Next, there is gambling. For many years, this was a subject that the church condoned, while at the same time the Catholic Church was the instigator of gambling. The church, every week, held bingo to raise money, if this is not gambling, what is?

Let's move on to the Mormons. This group, under the false umbrella of religion, is really a cult (organized crime). Once you are indoctrinated and brainwashed into this group, unlike the others, there is no other religion you would want to move to. First of all, the Mormons do not use the standard bible. They have their own version of a bible. Doesn't this give you a clue that something is not right? It's bad enough that the standard Bible is so far from the truth, now we go off in another direction called religion. The best I can see is this cult is still under control, not like Jimmy Jones. The Mormons, like organized crime, own many businesses. These businesses pay taxes to the state, but all of the profits go to their church. Isn't this the same principle that the mafia does? The only advantage of joining the Mormon cult is they do take a little better care of their members. This does not excuse them from keeping you under their control. The Mormon "Religion" has such a good brainwashing technique, and it has been going on for so long, that their members cannot see the forest for the trees in front of them. The leaders of this group have their followers coming behind them like a herd of sheep. The only good thing I can say, about this group (cult), is they do not waste as much money on the building as many other groups (faiths) do. And the major thing the Mormons do that is distasteful is in their brainwashing. They send the young members out to canvas neighborhoods looking for suckers to come and join their church. If their faith was so on track, why do they have to go out and recruit more sheep to their flock? Once you get hooked into their flock, it becomes much more difficult to be an independent thinker or person. The control in this group (cult) is so enormous, that once you're in, you don't want to leave.

Moving right along, we have the Baptist. This group has such an unrealistic view of religion, which in the area's that this faith is so strong; it is called the Bible Belt. The Baptist (cult) faith is so blind to reality that they try to chastise anybody that does not believe as they do. This group is so strong, that in the south they actually control the government. Where the Baptist are very strong, they make rules so that other faiths may attempt to follow suit. The Baptists follow the bible so closely; they have earned the name of Bible Bashers (a bible basher is someone who wants to force their belief onto you). I have watched the Baptist build an elaborate church and college in the last couple of years. But the waste of church money to build these fancy, elaborate buildings is very enormous. At the same time, I've seen very little help to poor and homeless. This group as well as many others would rather put their money into something to make man feel good. Not into humanity. This is the same as the organ, the dance, the music, and singing in the church. The only purpose of these items has nothing to do with religion or faith. They are there only to make each of us feel good about ourselves and allow us to relax.

We also have the Monks. These men go off and hide in search of the higher power, not quite ever reaching their goal. What a waste of human energy and resources.

I could continue on to many other faiths, but it would be redundant. My point is this, If we all start out the same as little children and end up with the same god, Why are there so many of man's versions of what religion or faith is? Why are wars fought over religion? As humans, we need a common ground for "Faith" and "Spirituality" so we can love thy neighbor, not fight. Also, why do most church's not allow women to be Priest's? Women have as much right as men to administer the teachings of god.

Just a simple note about control, when Beer was first developed and refined about the fifth century, the church was the one that maintained control of this substance for many years. Can you figure out why, money?

CHAPTER FIVE

RELIGION

This is one of the most incorrectly interpreted words that we have. Now we are getting down to the nitty gritty of our discussion. The main definition of religion is to "CONFORM". Such as, "I go to church religiously". This statement says it all. It says I conform to what I am told to do by the church. Let's take a small overview of "religion" around the world. Let's start with England and Ireland. The state controls the church, or does the church control the state? This war over religion has been going all on for so many years with no change in sight. When will the Crown of England denounce the religious part of their government? Ask anyone over the pond if the church and state are one, and your answer will be definitely no. When you get a no answer, ask what the Irish are fighting about. As I said before, this war will not end until the government gets out of religion.

If the church is a body of people, as Jesus described it. How can the church own a country in the name of religion? This was a ploy of the state many centuries ago to dupe people into believing they are not the same. Religion, always has been, and will continue to be until man breaks away from religion. Stop conforming to the control of the church in the name of religion. Be assured, I did not say to break away from god, just religion. Going a little farther east, the mid east countries have been at war with their neighbors for so many centuries, I don't think they can ever say when it started. Israel, the Jews have not had peace since as far back as time records go. These wars are always over religion. But the country has not always been called Israel. But these are the same people in the same area with the same ideas. Now move over to the area of Iran, Iraq, and Pakistan etc. This area of the world has changed country names after each war. Wars of religion, just as right now, all of the wars in this area are always over religion. The Koran controls its people much stronger than most religions. And they have a much stronger church/state. In these countries if you disobey the church, the state steps in and delivers the punishment. You steal, you loose a hand. You have pleasure with another man's wife, somebody dies. It seems almost every religion, or race has their own version of religion. The results are still the same, control. When man learns to reject religion, the control, and listen to his or her own god, wars will be a thing of the past. Religion must be crushed for man to move forward and have peace on earth. Just a reminder here, spirituality will replace religion. Let's take a look to Central America. If you follow any of the history channels, all of the scholars in many fields have one question not answered. Why the thriving civilizations of Central America that just up and vanished. That today, nobody seems to understand why. If you step back and take a good look with open eyes, it is very simple. This was a time when countries were moving around the world. The English, French, Spanish, etc, as these countries moved around and overtook different cultures, the Spanish, in their greed for wealth, did not understand the beliefs of a foreign religion. Therefore the Spanish forced Christianity on these people. If they did not conform to the ways of Christianity, the people were slaughtered like cattle. We must step back and take a new look at the situation. The Aztec culture thrived for many, many years. The Spanish came in and stole from these people. But what nobody seems to address, is the Spaniards stole much more than their material possessions. The Spaniards stole the Aztecs reason to live. They stole their spirituality. The major difference between this civilization and most others is the Spaniards forced the change overnight; therefore the Aztec's could not handle the change, whereas most of the world had centuries to adjust to a change. I honestly believe the Aztecs had a true religion, spirituality, as the American Indians have. I say again the American Indians

35

are the only race to maintain the true original spirituality of their forefathers. With an open mind of change, and what is a possibility of the past. IF, humanity got a little kick start from an alien race, the American Indian's are the only human race that still maintains the original alien language as other Indian races have. To backup the statement, go back to World War II. All languages were able to break the secret code of other languages except that of the American Indian. Therefore, during World War II, the American Indians were the only ones that other languages could not quite be understood, thus getting the name of "Code Talkers", and it still stands today.

If we want to get into more summation facts, let's go to the Orient. Now this is the area of the world where spacecrafts are also in their history. Let's look at the difference of these people from the rest of the world. They have their own way of life from everybody else. Suppose when our alien fathers gave us a kick start, that another alien race gave these people a kick start by intermingling with the people of that area. The people appear very different from the rest of the world, their language is also extremely different, but best of all, their religion and believes are extremely different, and nothing has changed their belief or spirituality over the centuries.

In simple words, civilized man is so brainwashed, that in most situations, he is closed minded to anything other than what he has been taught, right or wrong. In most situations if you cannot touch nor have hard proof that something exists, then it doesn't. If that is the situation, why does any man believe in God so strongly? There is no PROOF or HARD EVIDENCE that God does exist. To me, this is a major contradiction that man has created himself. If God does (which he does) exist, where is any hard proof? The travesty of what man's religion has done to himself by allowing the church elders to take control of our life.

Please don't misunderstand the meaning or direction of my message. There is no way that the present form of faith can be changed overnight. The severity of the religious brainwashing is so enormous and has been going on for so long, that first we must have a common understanding and believe in place, and in operation, before mankind can get rid of the control by the Church and State.

The Church does not need you to tithe, or give as much as you can (close to ten percent), except to build a fancy Temple or Cathedral and buying new cars, paintings, tapestry, stained glass windows, and etc. All of these things are material items that have nothing to do with God's world. They are pretty to look at, and that is part of the church's brainwashing, and its working.

If the church of today was to collapse right now, there are many people that need religion to hang onto, that this is a necessity in today's world. I am not professing that my words are the only way. There might be a better method than what I am being told at this time. What I am professing is that the church is part of the state. First, they must become separated. Second, man must start thinking for himself. Third, man must stop being controlled by the church and state. When man becomes free of control, then, and only then can he become self sufficient and industrious enough to expand his mind far beyond where he has gone so far. Don't continue to be stuck in a rut. Let's look to the future and move forward much faster than we have so far. Since we use only ten percent of our computer brain, we need to get rid of this control, think how much faster we can expand the use of our brain without the present brainwashing? Let's presume all humans get on the same path and stop fighting among ourselves in an animalistic manor, then, what would this world be like, all humans working together for one goal, to learn and grow? Then suppose that our Alien fathers came and said "HI", because now they would not fear being damaged or destroyed. Many people have asked if these spaceships are sent all the time, why don't they show themself? Mainly because, if they did today, our armies would attempt to kill them on contact based on fear, remember, this is about control. Our government and others have spaceships and much more info about Alien races. But this info is hidden from the general public. These government officials, in their control do not realize that the general public is much smarter than to fall into the trap of not receiving what is known by our Government officials, again control. Most governments use the excuse that national security is the reason that this information is held from its populace.

CHAPTER SIX

GOD

Let's start off in simplicity. There is no Theologian that I am aware of that will tell you who god is. They will attempt to give you their version based on what they have been taught by man. They are so brainwashed by the church and its doctrine, that if anyone ever figures out that the religious world is on the wrong track, they are afraid of being chastised by the rest of the world. I have met some ministers that after going through many years of Theology School and years of service in the church left the ministry because they finally understood that what they were teaching and reaching for was not the correct information. These men did not know or have the correct answer, but they could not continue to teach what they could not understand.

I'm going to try to approach this slowly, so what I have to say will make sense, so you can really understand the message that god has given me to pass on. Please proceed with an open mind. We have to squash the brainwashing in order to hear our god. Many, many people go to church religiously knowing there is more out their, but never getting an answer.

Before we go on, who is GOD? God is a collective of spirits or guides for each individual person that is comprised of your ancestors and their friends. Each person has their own personal god. Contrary to what the church (Religion) has been professing that god is an imaginary entity out there someplace that we cannot talk to or hear. How many of you can remember talking to a departed relative? The church tries to explain this side of spirituality as taboo so they may maintain their control.

In recent years there have been many new TV programs showing and proving that there are Spirits here and all around us. Most of the Spirits that the TV programs discover are people that had a hard time in this life, or died unexpectedly. Therefore, are having a hard time moving on. In a percentage of the world population, these spirits that remain behind are very, very small amount. Until that spirit gets their situation resolved, they cannot move on. But for the billions of spirits that move on to the next plane, or into god's world, life is marvelous. A spirit is something everybody has. It has been physically proven. Spirits or souls have been seen and weighed. So all of you skeptics, it is a proven fact that spirits do exist. I personally have seen a spirit. One Sunday morning, at church, after service, doing Holistic Healing on a India lady, half way thru the healing, the congregation, got my attention, only to see a spirit leave this Lady's body, float up and out the window. She then became totally relaxed (that was her reason to be there) and left the Church a different person.

Many, many people have experiences with spirits. Sometimes you know who comes to visit you, sometimes you don't. Next time when you get a smell that reminds you of someone that has passed on, say hello and acknowledge the fact that you recognize their presence. Do you realize your spirit ancestors, are with you for a reason? Either to confirm their acknowledgement of something you have done or maybe to help guide you to make a decision. Sometimes just to say hello. Most of the time, we will not know who the guides are that are here to help and us. Very few of us know who, or how many guides are with us at any time. Be assured you are never without at least half of your guides at any one time.

There is no such thing as one omniscient being or spirit, all knowing for everybody. God is our savior, our guide, and protector. Any time we feel that god has let us down or forsaken us, it is ourself that has given up on ourselves. Anytime anyone feels alone or without god, is the time when our god is carrying us. Please read the following copy to of the prayer.

"Footprints"

""One night a man had a dream. He dreamed he was walking along the beach with the LORD. Across the skies flashed scenes from his life. He noticed two sets of footprints in the sand. One belonging to him and the other to the LORD.

When the last scene of his life flashed before him, and he looked back at the foot prints in the sand. He noticed that many times on the path of his life there was only one set of footprints. He also noticed that it happened at the very lowest and saddest times in his life.

This really bothered him and he questioned the LORD about it. LORD you said that once I decided to follow you, you'd walk with me all the way. But I have noticed that during the most troublesome times in my life, there is only one set of footprints. I don't understand why when I need you the most you would leave me.

The LORD replied. My precious, precious child, I love you and I would never leave you during your times of trial and suffering. When you see only one set of foot prints, it was then that I carried you.""

Author unknown

Every person in this world is a unique individual. Every person has their own god, a collective of spirits and/or guides to try and guide you thru this lifetime. When you listen to your God, things will go well. Remember, God said he will give man a free will. So when you do not listen, and do things on your own, and then they don't turn out so good, who can you blame, but yourself? When you find yourself in a situation and hear yourself saying, God, I can't handle any more, you will have to look back on your life to see what YOU did wrong. God had nothing to do with it. Due to our brainwashing over life and church, sometimes we are unable to hear our God trying to guide us. Each person controls their own destiny. When you are able to slow down and hear your guides, and spirits, and you're God, things will start to be much easier. When I say to hear your god, I do not mean you will hear a voice, it will come to you in a feeling or thought that is very strong or out of text from what you normal thoughts are. When you get a very strong feeling or thought about something that you think is not normal, this will be your god speaking to you.

Please remember that GOD gave man a free will. When we are able to get our pride and ego out of the way and clear our mind so we can hear our God. You will find that things in life will go much smoother and more to our liking.

Now, did I get through to you? Who is God? This is the simplest question to answer, but the church will never tell you. If they did, the church will lose control and soon disappear. At this time, the brainwashing and money machine is too important for society to let go.

One more factor that must be explained, any child really has a better understanding of who God really is, but once we start to brainwash that child, he becomes confused. If everybody was true to themself, all we would need to teach a child is treat thy neighbor as thyself. As long as you do not harm your neighbor, the neighbor will do no harm to you. And this statement covers all Ten Commandments and any other law man has imposed on his parish. This is God's law, simple and clear, one rule for mankind.

All of the theories I've heard about, who, or what God is, have not made any sense. There are so many people that do not believe in God, because of whom, what, or where is this thing called God, that nobody has ever seen or touched, when in all reality they are talking about themself. As everybody has been told, God is omnipotent, all seeing, all knowing, and everywhere at all times. Put into reality that this is a 100 percent true statement. The only variation is so simple, each of us have our own god, now bring together a group of people and you now have God's together. Yes Plural, the more the people, the more Gods are now in a group. And as the saying goes, the more the merrier, or the more God's, the more powerful God is or God's are. Of all you people who say God does not exist, are in reality saying that you do not believe in yourself. Since each of us have our own God, and we are part of our own God, will each and every one of you start rethinking who we are!! As I said earlier, when we are proud of who we are as an Individual, just think, what we can accomplish without control from the church or state.

Something that must go along with this subject, Angels, in all reality are your Guides or Spirits. They are here to help each of us. They are the higher up Spirits, the ones that have progressed (more educated) to the level that they can come down to show their help, support, and guidance. Ask any child, before the brainwashing takes over, about Angels. A child has a better understanding of who God and Angels are before they are brainwashed. Carrying a symbol of an Angel is only a reminder to us, that we have our own Angel with us at all times. But praying to our Angel for personal gratification is a NO NO. This is why I hear so many people say that God is not listening to them. God and your Angels are here to help us with life, but not for personal gratification. Please keep in mind that Angels are part of God's Spiritual world, not part of Man's Religious world.

For all those people that say they don't believe in god or that god doesn't exist, please give this chapter a second chance to help you understand that what you are really complaining about is the church (organized crime) and NOT GOD. Since each of us has our own god, let's put our disbelief in the correct area and against the proper organization, Religion and the church. God is part of the Spiritualist group, but the church (religion) has incorporated God into their doctrine which makes it very difficult to understand or connect to. As I said earlier that god is part of each and every person which is the spiritual side of each and every one of us.

There are many people that are having experiences of seeing the Virgin Mary. These people are seeing an angel which is part of gods world. These experiences are the miracles of healing coming from gods world. Since many people do not understand gods world, the only way they can explain what they have seen is to give the experience a name such as The Virgin Mary. Nobody has said their vision actually identified itself as the Virgin Mary. All of these experiences are preformed by god's angels, by whatever name you want to attach to the wonderful experience. Thru the church's teachings the only name most people can associate with a miracle experience is The Virgin Mary.

CHAPTER SEVEN

INTUITION

This chapter is in all reality a continuation of the previous chapter. Intuition is one of the most misunderstood subjects in today's society. It is not a word spoken or a feeling to transverse between people. How many times are you asked a question and not even knowing the subject, the answer just comes to you. Watching a quiz show and answers just appear to you without previous knowledge of the subject. You have a decision to make and an answer is there on the tip of your tongue. Intuition most generally is referred to as a woman's intuition. Anybody and everybody have the same ability of intuition. Most men are taught to rationalize the situation first, even though they already have the answer. Intuition is the ability to open your mind and hear you're elders, or guides talking to you. I had a major problem with this for many years. I could hear and understand my guides, but I did not know at that time where the information was coming from. It took many years before this information made sense to me. Now if you want to talk about everything going wrong, and you ask, LORD what am I doing so wrong for this to happen to me? Or say, I can't handle any more. When you slow down enough and get your pride and ego out of the way. And then look back at your life and say why didn't I do this or that when I had the choice? The truth of the matter is you elected not to follow your first thought or intuition. In most cases this is the trait taught by man. Look at all options before making a rash decision. Most women will listen to their first thought or intuition.

This is one reason why when women were allowed to enter the business world that they move up the ladder a little faster. When every person learns to listen to his or her god (spirits or guides), things in this world will move much smoother. When mankind learns to listen to their god, guides, or spirits, there will be a lot less grief in the world. People won't have to look back and say "I should have done that instead of this". When you have a feeling of how to do something or what to do, then go with the first thought. It will almost always be the correct decision because almost always, it is your god speaking to you. When you learn to get it right, from god and not mans thinking, you will be on the right track ninety-nine percent of the time. Now get it right, listen to your God, you're intuition, and have a much happier life.

On the Bio Channel, a program dated July 21, 2008, about Physic kids, will explain more of this. For a visual explanation of what I am trying say, view a copy of the movie "**Ghost**" staring Patrick Swayze and Whoopi Goldberg.

CHAPTER EIGHT

PRAYER

By all rights, I feel this is something, in most situations, that man has created to make himself feel good. In a few times of use it is to reach god for help. The first major problem, when people pray is the folded hands, "PRAYING HANDS". God is an energy spirits. When I pray, you will not find my hands folded. What you will find, is my hands will be turned, palms up, to give and receive the energy of the universe. How do you expect to be received, when you close one of the major areas of thought energy to transpire? This is the same as when someone is talking to you, telling you something and you fold your arms across your front. When you fold your arms across your front, a block has just been created and rejecting any and all information that you should be receiving. This is exactly the same thing that is done when the hands are folded (closed).

Another major fault with man's prayer is bowing the head in prayer. There are the faiths that also cover the head, same difference. When I pray, I lift my head high, proud to be one of God's children. Not ashamed of whom I am. If you ever find me praying, I'll have my hands turned up, my head high, proud to be a child of god.

What I've found over many years, is the average person, abuses prayer. When you abuse prayer, it now becomes a worthless waste of time. If you will now remember, I said, god is you and your ancestors. And therefore if you think using prayer as a pawn for your own personal gain, think again, because you are only fooling yourself.

My definition of prayer is very simple. Please remember, under god, it is very clear. There is only one rule. Do not do unto others you don't want done to you. I want to live my life like a prayer. That means that every night when I go to bed, I do not have to ask for forgiveness of something I did today. Therefore, I don't sit down and pray every night like most people. In simple words, quit fooling yourself. Live your life so as never to ask forgiveness from yourself and your god.

When three or more people hold hands and prey it is a prayer vigil, you have all of your god's together for a main purpose that is very effective.

Now let's get down to the true meaning of prayer. Prayer is designed to reach out and help. In all reality, prayer is ineffective from one person. A true prayer is what is referred to as a prayer vigil. Let me refresh. God is many for each person. Now a prayer vigil is many people getting together and asking for help. So let's look at the overall picture. Many people bringing together many, many guides. The more guides, the stronger the prayer is. This is true prayer. Please remember, one is weak, many are strong, the more the many, the stronger the prayer. In simple words, prayer is not to forgive your daily sins, you must learn to live in such a manner that daily or weekly forgiveness is not a way of life. This is one area the present church does good, on Sunday morning when a mass or congregation prey as a group.

CHAPTER NINE

MEN OF THE CLOTH

This is one of the saddest things that has happened to man today. These people are so deep into what the bible says; they cannot see the forest for the trees. Any true Theologian will tell you that the bible is a storybook. But at the same time, they try to explain what this story means. Every minister will read a passage out of the bible and give you a different meaning or variation. A story is just that, a story. There are many faiths out there that also recognize only certain passages out of the bible while ignoring other messages (mans control). I am not picking on any one faith, but looking at an example. The Mormon faith is very strong and I give them our recognition for their strength. But why do they use a different bible than most Christians? This is not the only faith that uses their own version of the bible. All of this strength and control comes from their faith leaders. These men believe so strongly that their faith is better than all the others, that when on the pulpit, they can convince their followers that this is the only way. This pastor will convince you, if you don't follow his teachings, you are on your way to damnation and hell. The truth is that HELL is life here on earth.

In most areas of the country, gambling is illegal. When the church wanted to raise money, the first thing they did was start a Saturday bingo (which is gambling) and it was approved by the state. Again, the church has first control. One of the largest lies of the Catholic Church is the priest and nuns cannot marry because they are married to the church. This allows the priest and nuns to fornicate within the church walls. One of their major sins that the perish is not supposed to do. Isn't this what was done in the past by the Pharaohs? This practice also has to stop. Also in recent years, the Catholic Church has paid out enormous amounts of money to keep quiet all of the problems of pedophile and sex offenders that their priests and church officials have done. They have a habit of moving priests from one area to another so as to cover up a problem.

In recent times, there are more and more priests, nuns, and the ministers leaving their faith due to the fact that they are learning more about the truth and less about what they have been taught.

The Baptist are no different. They go at the subject of brainwashing the children at an age before the baby can understand or reason. That means to the priest or church, says now I have got you for life because I brainwashed you before you could think for yourself. I watched a Baptist church and college being built over recent years. A grand chapel, housing and teaching facilities to compare to some of the finest hotels around, looking at the expense this faith has gone to, to provide for their future priests is amazing. And to think, all this money is actually stolen from the followers in the name of god, when god had nothing to do with the process.

If you were to go overseas to many of the mid east countries, you would find that their faith or priest actually runs the country. The man of the cloth in many countries has more power than they're elected officials. The thing you don't see is what goes on behind closed doors. How the officials change the rules so as not to loose control.

Going back to the catholic faith, the pope is a man who controls millions of people. In reality he is only a man who, if he knows who god is, will not tell the masses or he will lose all of his control. I doubt very much if the pope really understands the full power he has. I also, very much doubt if the pope really knows who god is.

We, as a group, need to find a way to reduce the power and control that the leaders of every faith have over their followers.

Another fact that is not in plain view, any minister that has good charisma and raises the financial status of his perish, this minister will be promoted to a larger perish to raise larger amounts of money for the church body. This appears to me the same as the Mafia does, to raise money for the main organization.

Now there is the Jewish faith. Can anybody tell me why the Jewish people do not recognize Jesus Christ? Ask any Rabi his opinion on this subject! All faiths that I am aware of believe in Jesus except the Jewish faith. Since Jesus was a Jew, why do the Jewish people not believe that he was our savior, only just another man? There seems to be major variation in thought between the Jews, Catholic, Protestant and Muslim Faiths. Can anybody tell me why? Could this be that since the church is controlling man, not god and the rules were made by man's idea for control?

One of the major things that bothers me, if you study what Jesus said, how can so many people use a "Preacher of Religion" as a profession when only your belief in god is all you need? Being a Minister or preacher was originally started as a position in the Pharaoh's court, not a profession. Is this not the same as the Mafia? A major organization for control and profit.

CHAPTER TEN

SPIRITUALITY

I have been explaining spirituality in every chapter. I believe that I am not telling you to do anything that has not been done or said in the past. What I want is for everybody to open their eyes, your minds eye and look at the possibilities that are available to every human being. All of the facts are available if you can see through all of the brainwashing that has been going on for centuries. Is the human race going to continue to allow this travesty to continue? Being led around like a herd of cattle? Saying yes sir and not questioning what or why we are being told the things that are important for the survival of life. If everybody had more interest in their well being, instead of let's say, sports. Do you realize just how much time and money is wasted on sports instead of being productive for each of our own future? Do you have a dream? What are you doing to chase your dream, are you putting any effort into bettering yourself? Or do you just sit back and say, I would like to do whatever your dream is. Or do you just sit back, watching a bunch of guys, who found their dream, chase a ball around a big field making big bucks. Do you realize that sports is actually another form of control, following sports instead of paying attention to what is happening to your life around you? If you take a serious look at sports, you will discover that sports is a method of control so people will not pay attention to what the powers to be are doing to your life. Sports are supposed to be a method to relax, not a way of life.

In simple words, spirituality is about you. You control yourself. Now how much effort do you expend on yourself? Not just appearance, but what is done to improve your future. Do you feel like you are proud of yourself? Can you honestly say "I am somebody"? Do you feel like you are putting an effort into your future, or do you feel like each day is repetitive, just to put food on the table? There are so many people that spend hours to make themselves look good right now, then go to the dinner table and become a glutton, not caring about how they look tomorrow. The United States population has become grossly overweight, not because Americans care about themselves or about the future. Again, much of this problem started in childhood. Parents that didn't care about themselves, forced this attitude on their children, so when they grew up they don't know any better. It takes a complete reprogramming to undo the stupidity that has been pushed onto us as children, the same as in religion, early brainwashing. Only when man rationalizes that he is the only one that controls his own life and future, can we as a whole body move forward and advance.

Let's review what's been covered. Spirituality is what man needs, not religion. That we are not meant to be like cattle and follow the leader. Each of us is our own god. Our ancestor spirits and guides are with each of us at all times. Therefore our god to each of us is all knowing at all times. Isn't this so simple, that the church and religion don't want you to know because then they would lose control of the masses.

After many centuries, don't you think it's time that man takes control of his own life and stops letting himself be controlled by someone else?

For all of you people that have that feeling that there is something else out there, something better than you have been told. Could spirituality be what you have been searching for? Only you can make a decision of what is in store for your future. You have been told all your life what's right for you and what you must do. Don't you think it's about time you think for yourself? It's time you do what you feel is right and good for yourself in your heart. The writer of this book is not telling you to do anything. I am only asking you to look at your life vary seriously and very deeply. And then make your own decision of where you want your life to go.

If you want an example of how man has been held back, just look at the human brain. We use only about ten percent of our brain which is the largest computer on the earth. If you went out and purchased a computer and it was only ten percent efficient, would you be satisfied? Then why are we all satisfied with the control, we as humans have been under. THINK FOR YOUR SELF PEOPLE.

There are many groups of faith that say they are spiritual or groups that say they are non denominational. Both of these groups are about the same. But for the most part, these groups of faith are saying that there is something else, much greater out there, but due to what I call sideways brainwashing, they are confused and searching for a solid answer.

Let me explain sideways brainwashing. Sideways brainwashing is when you see, hear, and read, all about a subject without any proof of its validity. And all of the followers are doing the same thing. But there is no proof that they are right or wrong. All of the spiritual groups that I have been involved with also have a hard time being very definite as to who god is. They do mostly understand that there is no hell as the organized religion tries to cram down our throat. Most do realize that hell is right here on earth with all of us. I have met many people that do not believe in religion as the church tries to tell us. But almost every one of these people, do believe in a higher power—"God". This is a very large group that is extremely spiritual, not religious, but looking for something that will make sense of their faith. If the words in this book help anyone understand what your faith is all about, as my guides and god's have told me to put into words. As I said earlier, there is only one law in the spirit world, except for one thing. Gluttony is disrespecting yourself and your god. The one law is "Do onto others as you would have them do onto you". The Ten Commandments all fall under this one law. But when it comes to not respecting yourself, how can you respect anybody, anything or your god? You must respect yourself first. Your body is a temple to your god. Please do not misunderstand my statement. There is a major difference between being large framed and being overweight. I have a friend who considers herself fat, when in all reality, she is only a large framed person. Now, the fact is that many overweight people started as a child. Their parents overweight have forced this trait on to their children. When this situation occurs, these people will have a hard time reversing the childhood brainwashing. Spirituality starts with loving thy self first, are you proud of whom you are? Not of what you have accomplished, or where you have gotten in society, but are you proud of whom you are as a person. When you look into a mirror, can you say, I am proud of who I am, I am proud of how I look? Your body in all reality is a temple to your god. Can you say to yourself and the world—"I AM SOMEBODY"? And mean it 100%? As a person in god's world, in order to advance in the spirit world, you must be proud of yourself, you must be proud of your god. God does not make ugly people, only man does. God does not make dummies, but man does create such. So let's look back inside each of us and help thy neighbor to make this a better place to live. In the Gospel of Thomas, Jesus said we are all children of god. Therefore, we answer to no one but our own private god.

Something to be aware of, there are some people that will try to use spirituality as a way to rob you. Don't fall prey to individuals that work as an independent, Out of their house or store front. If they don't belong to a spiritualist church or group, be very aware of them asking for large amounts of money. If you do want to visit a person for a reading, or similar, do not tell them anything, only let them tell you whatever there message is, and complete it, before answering anything and keep a good poker face. A good con artist can take a simple statement, gesture or answer to a question and give a pat answer that will fit almost anyone. When a reader asks a question, just say go on, and wait until they finish before acknowledging anything. But if you have told them something and their answer sounds perfect to your situation, just be aware. Keep a poker face with a reader for best results.

Crystal balls, cards, Palm readers, and any other form where they do this for a living, and have a storefront are generally a fraud. These $20.00 readings are for entertainment only. There are many professional people that do this for a living, that are honest and true, so just be aware of who you are using.

CHAPTER ELEVEN

JESUS AND U. F. O'S

This is one of the major subjects that will receive major criticism. Everybody must learn to have an open mind. The church has done such a great job of brainwashing, which the average person (in any faith) cannot see beyond their nose. If you don't agree or understand that statement, go back and read again, only to be able to open your mind and look at all or only some of the options available to mankind, MEANING YOU.

Pyramids and are generally thought of to be around Egypt, only because they are easily seen and of the largest ever built. So now let's go to Mexico, South America, North America, Scotland, China, Japan, and many other locations. There are pyramids all over the world. Since nobody today really knows the purpose or function of pyramids that were built so long ago, that there is no record of many of these structures. Example—a pyramid built of earth in the Saint Louis Missouri area which has disappeared. If these structures were built by our ancestors, why don't we have any record of why, or who built them. The earliest pyramids were constructed of material that would not hold up to the weather like the later stone structures. The other subject that goes along with this, is who built the pyramids, this is a major question. Many archaeologists think that the Egyptians built the stone pyramids. If this is true, why are all of the Pharaoh's buried in the Valley of the Kings, and not the in the pyramids. They find drawings on the walls, trying to say that these were built by the Egyptians. I believe that as time goes on, they will find out that these pyramids were built by a much earlier race.

UFOs and the government are one of the biggest jokes of today. As far back as archaeologist can trace man, there are cave drawings. If cave drawings are many thousands of years old, and in these cave drawings have pictures of UFOs. That means these flying machines have been around for thousands of years. If this is the situation, how gullible does the government think we are? In this situation the state again is working on controlling what we think. They are the stupid ones. UFOs are in all of recorded history. Why is the state so ignorant as to try and hide the fact that UFOs are here, and have always been here? Many people feel and know that these aliens are watching us and have vowed not to interfere with the development of the human race. Scientist say there's no hard evidence of UFOs, so they do not exist. Well drawings of these flying ships have been around for thousands of years. The bible even has many stories about flying ship, why do we need any more proof? These flying ships vary in size and shape. Due to the variation of UFO's observed in today's times, indicates that there are more than one alien race keeping track of the human race. Humans are such a violent race; I believe these aliens are just making sure that we do not bring our violence out into their world. If you look at all of the humans on the earth, the different races have such a variation in appearance and stature. If the aliens did jumpstart the humans on earth, it indicates that more than one alien race has been here to help the humans get started.

Now let's go back about 2,000 years. If you study the history books around that time, it appears that greed, gluttony, and violence was on a rampage, and in all appearances, getting out of control. So it appears that the alien race saw a need to interfere with human progress. This was not the first time. We will get to that a little later. But for now, how could the other race help humans with the least amount of interference? It came to be that they would send one of their own to try and help guide us into the future. Mother Mary bore a child without being with a man (as the bible says). Today we have many records of women being pregnant and their baby just disappearing from their body after a few months, and a couple years later being reunited on a spacecraft with a child being told that this is their child. With as many sightings and reports about UFO aliens, is this so far fetched? Next question, at the time of the birth of Jesus, three wise men followed a shining star to his birthplace. Who were these three wise men? Where did they come from? These three wise men brought great wealth with them and placed it at the foot of the manger. If this was true, Joseph would have been a rich man and would not have had to work. What happened to all the riches bestowed on Jesus when he was born? Since Mary was a virgin, who was the father of Jesus? It seems very possible that Jesus was half human and half another race, such as Alien. Therefore was Jesus half alien, and half human? This would help explain why he has been the only one known to humanity to, by a touch, heal the human body, or by a gesture, start a fire, or create rain, etc. Now going back, the three wise men followed a bright shining star. The Star of Bethlehem. I don't think so. There has never been any recording of such a thing to ever happen before or after this incident. Let's look from reality. The bright shining light could have been from a UFO announcing to the world that they had a special person being born. Also, after the birth of Jesus, where did the three a wise men go? Why did we not here anything else about the trio? What, you say this is a little too far fetched to be true. Then let's go back to the time of the pyramid building. This is another time when the alien fathers did mankind a boost. All of these stories of hundreds of men moving rocks that man has no way of moving today is much more far fetched. Also, when the pyramids were being built, how did they get two fifty ton rocks to fit so perfectly, that even today, you cannot get a piece of paper to fit between them. Our ancestors at that time, being greedy, so afraid of losing their power and control, that this knowledge did not get passed on, or got lost. It only took a handful of men to move that large a stone. To back up that statement, look up the Coral Castle in Florida, USA in the early nineteen hundred's. When one man without any equipment, would move a 5 ton piece of Coral, also, he cut and lifted that five ton piece of Coral out of a quarry by himself. This man also died without passing on the knowledge of the universe of how he did it.

There are pyramids all over the world. Nobody ever talks about how these other pyramids were built. You have the same scenario, every place pyramids were built. Also there are figures In South America (nasca lines) that can only be seen from far up in the sky. They are so old that there is no record of how old they are or who built them.

Are we as human beings so controlled that if we can not put our hands on solid proof that these things don't exist? Then the skeptics have their way when the evidence is right In front of you. We each have a brain, so lets use it.

Something else, if you go back to the bible and read Exodus much closer about Moses and Mt. Sinai, you will find a direct reference to aliens or UFO's. Also you will find that direct reference in Ezekiel and 2Kings. Then read Act's about how St. Peter was released from jail by an Angel (or an alien).

Before we leave this subject, there is one more thing that must be explained. There are many stories in history, and some of the stories are called mythology. Due to our brainwashing, is very hard to understand what any of the stories mean. All of our scientist and archaeologist say that if you do not have hard proof, it is just a story. Therefore they are untrue. Let's go back in time and take a hard look at Greek mythology. If you go back and read much of the Greek Mythology, you will discover that they had flying saucers coming quite often. These stories are truer than anybody realizes. In those days the people did not know of alien races, they only knew about their gods. When you read Greek mythology, they talk about the gods coming and taking wives. With an open mind, you will realize that their gods were actually aliens. The stories were deemed as mythology because they seemed too far fetched for man to understand or believe. With what we know today, the stories are not that far fetched as our ancestors believed. Also, if you read some of the Edgaer Cayce books, which he explained much of this to be true. There is so much that we do not understand, or have no proof of from the past, that we must use our brainpower and reasoning to break through the brainwashing that the church and state has been putting on us. As time goes on in the future, more of this will be understood with some sort of validity to backup what is not known at this time. Right now we know more about space than we do our own planet. There are too many unknowns for us not to accept the possibility of what happened in the past, because the archaeologists are still uncovering facts and learning so much more of what used to be. We must break the brainwashing process and start using our minds to proceed with life. Governments around the world are hiding the facts of UFOs and USOs in the name of national security, denying that they exist, but they do have some of the alien technology that we are not supposed to know about. This is some of the control the church and state are putting on us that we must eliminate.

For more info on our government and UFOs on the internet, look up on the History Channel a program that aired on Feb. 25, 2009. UFO Hunters, area 51 revealed. How the government is working on reverse engineering the UFOs that they have at area 51 in Nevada, also the program that aired on March 08, 2009, Program on Ancient Aliens.

While we are talking about UFO's, a program on the HINT Channel (History International), aired on July 25, 2005. Talks about the USA Presidents knowledge and observation of UFOs, but how they were advised not to speak about the subject, is this control? Also on the HINT channel, title Ancient Aliens, originally aired on Oct. 11, 2000 and History Mysteries, also May 18 2010 and Oct 28 2010.

Let's go to the bible for more related information. Genesis 6:4, Exodus 14:21-28, Exodus 19:16-21, 2 Kings 2:11-16, Ezekiel 10:6-22. These are some of the stories that are talking about the aliens they witnessed. Read between the lines to understand what those people saw and how they explained what they had seen. At the time these stories were written, the people did not know about aliens, only the gods. Therefore, they explained what they saw as gods, not what really happened.

CHAPTER TWELVE

CHRISTMAS AND EASTER

Now we're getting into new territory. If Christmas is suppose to celebrate the birth of Jesus Christ, but the church fathers back at the time, did not think the simple celebration was good enough. But as I said in chapter nine, the church elders created a story of the three wise men with very expensive jewels, gold, and much more. These wise men appeared from nowhere and left the same way. There was no cache of gold and gifts. This is this why Joseph did remain a poor man? If this story was true, Joseph would have been a rich man. In my estimation, this story was created and carried through to today for profit for the church elders. But in those days, the gift of Christmas was a crucifix, or just a cross that was controlled by the church to make money. Isn't that what has become of Christmas today. The Stores started advertising products three or four months early for Christmas, nothing about god or Jesus, just money. Also due to the commercial hype, those retailers have crossed Christ out of Christmas, "Xmas". Damn that person.

Christmas is supposed to be a sharing of love and yourself to others in the name of god, for peace and harmony in the world as the church tells us. But instead of love, it has become a commercial buying frenzy. In my opinion, the organized church (organized crime) still promotes the commercial side of Christmas for profit. Just look at how many trees are cut down in the name of religion. There are many stores that if it was not for Christmas buying, they could not keep their doors open. The simple fact that "Xmas" was started as a commercial promotion, this is a positive sign that the general public has lost the true meaning of Christmas. And damn that person for helping the general public forget what Christmas Is really about. Due to previous, as a child's brainwashing, many people go to church on Christmas and Easter because they feel an obligation. The biggest problem is these people go to church only two days a year and they really don't know why or understand what Christmas is all about.

Then there is Santa Claus. This is a great fictional figure for the children. But the problem with Santa Claus is really very simple. This is promoting the commercial side of the holiday. It is reinforcing the brainwashing to a child, and not educating the children to the truth. Therefore many people do not understand the true meaning of Christmas. But what the average person understands about Christmas is money and gifts, and not love from the heart. How many gifts are given as an obligation, and not from the Heart?

Something else the Church did, when calculating what day Jesus was born many years later, they goofed. Jesus was not born on December 25. Nobody really knows what day Jesus was born. What is the significance of Dec. 25. Could it be Astrology??

And now, how about Easter, since when is Easter a fashion show? Again, this is one of the holiest days of the year. Why is this day clouded with the new and fanciest clothes? As long as I have been on this earth, Easter has been a commercial clothing day. Go buy your new spring clothes so you can go to church and show them off. You spend days or weeks preparing your spring's wardrobe, and then spend one or two hours with the father. This is a day of celebration, but very little time is spent on Jesus Christ and what this day is about. Ask many people what the true meaning of Easter is, and you will be surprised at the answers you will get.

Easter is like Christmas. Easter has the Easter bunny. Now can you tell me what the Easter Bunny and colored eggs have to do with Jesus Christ or god? When are we going to face reality? Yes, the Easter egg hunt is great for the children, but we must teach our children what Easter is truly about. The only plausible answer to who Jesus Christ is, I explained earlier. So what is the true purpose of Easter?

Easter is the Resurrection of Jesus Christ. This is the celebration of Jesus going home. Nobody knows what happened to the body of Jesus after his death. Also at that time, everybody wanted to know how that large stone was moved. If you use a little common sense, the disappearance of Jesus body and the moving of the stone to the entrance to the crypt, is a very simple explanation. Jesus had his burial on earth, now it was time for his body to go home and have a proper burial with his other people and his father. In the Gospel of Peter, he tells the story of the Romans guarding the tomb of Jesus, watching the stone being moved and Jesus, with two other persons, ascending up into the clouds (to a UFO?). Jesus also said he would only give the Romans his body, so his spirit could go home. What is the true date of Easter, could this also be from Astrology??

We must start teaching our children the true meaning of Christmas and Easter first, and then we can have Santa Clause and the Easter Bunny as a child thing, not the true meaning. These are the Holist days of the year. Let's reinforce this to our children!!

Something else to consider, December 25 is the first day after the Winter Solstice and Easter is the day of the Spring Equinox.

CHAPTER THIRTEEN

REINCARNATION

Let's start by explaining actually what the soul or spirit are. Your soul or spirit are the same thing. Everybody's spirit is equal to another person within you that is an integrated part of each of us which is our energy intelligence that has been here before in another persons body.

Reincarnation is a subject that is well understood in the spiritualist group. Reincarnation is not what the average person understands. This is when a spirit returns to this plane to learn. How many times in history has there been a child prodigy? This is when a spirit is able to bring with him the memory of the past life or lives. There is no other explanation that makes sense to have such knowledge or talent. Every person on earth has been here before. How do you explain déjà vu? I've been here before, when in this life, you have never been to an area or ever read about it. Every spirit is of a higher power than the human form. The difference is very simple to many who understand the chain of command or order. Life on this plane is nothing more or less than a classroom. You are here to learn your lesson, if not, you will keep coming back until you can learn the lesson you have chosen to know, until you can pass the test. Every spirit also has a free choice. In the spirit world or next plane, it is much like here on earth. The further you want to advance, the more times you would need to return. The same as here on earth, if you want to advance in this world, first you graduate from high school, and then if you want a better job, you go to college for further education. This is exactly what happens in the spirit world, when you, as a spirit, decide to further yourself, you choose what lesson you need next. And then you have a choice of whom you will be and where your lesson will take place. But once you decide on the next lesson, you cannot give up until you get a passing grade or in other words you must learn the necessary lesson. Many people have the wrong idea about reincarnation. It is a free choice, the same as in this world, that, if you want to grow, you must go to school. There are all different kinds of schools. As god told man, you have a free will, it is also true in the spirit world, you have a free will to stagnant or move foreword.

The University of Virginia has studied over 2500 cases of reincarnation and has documented proof that Reincarnation is Real. When a person dies and their Soul moves on, only to return to this plain in another body, and sometimes the new person is able to remember many facts of the previous life. Other times only under hypnosis can the person remember facts of their previous life!. If you are able to get a copy of Edgaer Cayce's information about the original spirits to this planet, it will explain much of this. There was a program on the SYFY channel March 12, 2008 that shows proof of how Spirits come back to learn again.

Purgatory is actually a part of reincarnation. When a spirit has a hard time learning a particular lesson, or has a major situation in this life, that spirit loses track of their purpose here on this plane. Then when it's time to go home, they are totally confused and cannot let go of this life. Therefore, when the body dies and the spirit separates, it is totally lost and unable to move forward, back home. So it is lost halfway between our world and the spirit world. In many cases, if and when the disastrous situation is resolved, or the spirit realizes their mistake, then that spirit can go home.

For information see HINT channel. Science of the Soul that aired on Dec 19, 2010

CHAPTER FOURTEEN

THE DEVIL—LUCIFER

Before we get started the fact that Satan prior to 100AD, it was a know fact that Satan was not a person. Satan was a term used to describe a feeling or attitude. Then when Christianity got started, the church propagated the stories about Satan as a real person so they would have more control over their followers.

This is the most exaggerated story the church ever dreamed up. Let's go back to the chapter of god and look hard at who god is. In order to control the peasants back then, the church dreamed up the concept that anything that has gone wrong, somebody else caused it. Doesn't that make it easy? Now we have the concept, we do not have to take blame for anything we do that is wrong. He just says the devil made me do it. This now gives the church more power and control over their followers. This also created in mans imagination all of the things that would be totally distasteful for man's existence. All you have to do is look at all the variations of drawings of what Hell could look like if it were real. The devil is some creature that enjoys torture. This was the easiest way at that time the church could think of to control its masses. This Devil, Hell scenario scared the people into submission at a time before the average person was well educated. When more people became educated, the church started to lose control. Lucifer, a fallen angel started his control as the devil. But, if each of us is our own god, how can there be a fallen angel from god's graces? All of the portraits depicting what Hell is are one of man's greatest abilities, his imagination. Please be aware, that hell is what you make it to be. You control your own hell on earth. When you make a choice to cheat, steal, take another person's mate, or anything you do to harm your neighbor, you are creating a situation for yourself that in the future you will be very unhappy with. And thus, Hell On Earth, Now you must take responsibility for your own actions and stop blaming a none existent entity.

Now, if you go way back in time, before the time of Jesus, the original story was that Lucifer sat beside god. When god wanted to test the faithfulness of a person, The bible says that god would send Lucifer to do the dirty work, to put somebody thru nasty tests. Now do you see how the church turned this around to make Lucifer the devil? The church created the devil to sustain control! Can you imagine your god testing you to see how true you are to yourself? Do you now see how the church has changed things and created stories to keep the populous under control?

When you read the bible, about Jesus going off into the desert alone to test if he is the righteous one, and the devil followed him, who wrote the story if Jesus went off alone? If you will remember, god gave man a free choice. The whole story about the devil is so that man will chose the right path. Do you want to do the right thing? Not to harm thy neighbor? Or did you choose the wrong path for self gratification? I have met people today that say they have seen the devil. This one of man's greatest abilities, due to the brainwashing we have received, to create in our mind a deity that does not exist. With our computer brain, we can create almost anything. This is another reason that the control and brainwashing from the church must be stopped as soon as possible. We all have the ability to think for our self, so let's get it done. Something else of interest is Halloween which originally was a Pagan Ritual. As time went on and the meaning of Halloween changed, the church got involved and embellished the stories and propagated them to what they are today. The Jack-o-lantern was named after person, the original was a Turnip in the old country which in America became the pumpkin. Trick or treat only got started in America in the early 1900's.

For more information on the History Channel see Afraid of the Dark aired on July 6, 2010 and Real Story of Halloween aired on Oct. 26, 2010.

CHAPTER 15

EXORCISM

Before we go on, lets define what creates a situation that requires an exorcism. This situation occurs when a person has two or more spirits with them. Their own is of a positive attitude and the second spirit is of a negative attitude. Most people have only one spirit as their guide, but on occasion a negative or second spirit will invade a persons body trying to gain control. When this happens it requires some action to chase the negative spirit back to where it came from and give that person some peace. The church has defined this process as an exorcism.

This subject is totally misunderstood. The church defines this subject as the devil has entered somebody's body. As stated in the previous chapter, the devil is a figment of imagination created by the church. Now when the church conducts an exorcism, they usually conduct the service with only a few Priests in attendance. Now lets go to many churches that are not ordinary, or do not follow the ordinary method of preaching the Scriptures. In these churches many times you will see a form of exorcism being performed and accomplished. When these churches perform this service there are many people in attendance.

To be realistic in how to get rid of the second spirit is very different than what most people have been taught or told. Reminder, Psalms 118:8 It is better to put your trust in the Lord than put your confidence in man. What it takes to remove this spirit is not a cross or holy water, it takes many people with all their gods as explained in Chapter 8, a prayer. When a Priest does this service there are very few gods with him. A priest is following the Religious form and not the Spiritual form. When a Minister with his congregation are all praying at the same time, they have brought all their gods together at the same time, the results are now very affective and accomplish what is needed to remove the negative spirit. As stated in Chapter 6, with the guidance of my spirits, I have seen this accomplished with great results. This is the spiritualist results, not religion.

There are many people with an illness that the medical profession calls Schizophrenic. When a person has more than one visible personality, could it be possible that instead of an illness that the person is in possession of more than one spirit within them? Without all the brainwashing from the church and with some spiritual guidance, maybe there is an answer that has not been investigated yet. The only time the church gets involved is in extreme cases. Now, what about all the cases that are not extreme? When a person has a mental or physical problem, they go to a doctor looking for help and answers and what do they get, more medicine (chemicals). Now most doctors that have a religious background have another path to consider. Since the medical profession is still learning a lot about human body and brain, could there be another path of treatment for these people that has never been looked at? Instead of the devil, could these people have two or more spirits with them that are fighting each other and need spiritual help to relieve the problem? Since I have personally experienced this situation taking place, lets stop the brainwashing of the church and take a new spiritual look at the problem. Could many of the people with a Schizophrenic diagnosis have multiple personalities, when they hear voices or lose connection with reality. This sounds to me like there is more than one spirit within each of these people. Could a spiritual, laying on of the hands, in a large group of people, with all of their gods present help? Don't you think it is worth a try to put our trust into the Lord and not man? The more of us that turn to spirituality instead of religion, maybe this human race can start to help each other without fighting.

CHAPTER SIXTEEN

BIBLE BASHERS—DO GOODERS

My interpretation of a Bible Basher is somebody that tries to force their views of what the bible says onto somebody else without a full understanding of what they are reading and trying to force their beliefs onto somebody else.

Just for example, there are the Jehovah's Witnesses and the Baptist. If you people want to come to my door on Sunday morning to preach the bible, at least read the entire bible. When I was younger, I had these people come to my door reading this fabulous storybook, but because they did not read or understand all of the stories, I was able to recite another story that would contradict any story they could come up with. What about the people that go around with the bible closed and recite passages out of the good book, as if there were no other option. Wake up people, there are many faiths today that will tell you that the bible is just that, a story book. The only problem is these faiths still have a hard time explaining the reality and difference between religion and spirituality, because they don't know or understand it themselves. Then there are those that sing and dance in church. It makes me feel good that people enjoy who they are and what they believe in. The problem is they recognize their god on Sunday and forget about god all week long, only to repeat this every week. Again I say, be true to yourself and not some idol or false God.

Something else that has been misinterpreted. These groups go around bashing pornography with an unreal interpretation of this subject. Nudity does not fall into this category. The Human body is a "work of art" by our god. You need to read Webster's dictionary for an accurate definition of Pornography, and stop adding your personal version of what Pornography is. Pornography is the display of sexual acts only, and does not includes nudity. If you go back in time prior to today's religion, you will find many statues and paintings showing nudity. These works of art were and still are considered art. How did the church change art into something vulgar?

Now is there any place in the scriptures that says or spells out a list of vulgar or curse words? Not to my knowledge. But Bible Bashers get on a rampage in controlling cities or whole counties in the name of Jesus Christ. This is control from the church? I could go on and on, but I'll give only one other example. Let's go to the original faith (Jewish—as best as I can understand) and look at how different, but with the same control. They cover their heads (in shame) so as not to receive the energy of the universe. My point is very simple. If we all have our own individual god, why does every faith have a different set of rules? Do you really believe that each group of people has a different god? If not. Let's get together with one god and one set of rules.

If any of what I have said so far makes any sense to you, let's get together to free mankind of this ridiculous control. It is so antiquated, old, and out dated, that the brainwashing has to be stopped. As I said much earlier, the only true spiritual faith that I know of is the American Indians, also I believe that their language is of the original, possible from our alien father's.

It is very difficult for me to believe how many people take the bible as true gospel. The books of the bible are nothing more than stories of somebody's life. And they were intended for man to use as an example to guide us through life. The first book of the old testament talks about Adam and Eve. There are many faith groups that still take this story today as if it actually happened. This again was a story interpreted by the church fathers in an attempt to keep the people under control. The story of Adam and Eve was passed down for about 2000 years before the old testament was written. The bible and the Koran both have this story, but they very completely differ due to passed down versions of the story. The original story was of a man called Gilgamesh that occurred about 2000 years before the scriptures of Genesis were written. Now we are talking about control and brainwashing. Does this help you understand what the message of this book is about?? Also, in the bible, it states that Adam had another mate before Eve. Will you please explain that based on what the bible tells you? In other words, many stories in the bible are tales passed down thru time that contradict each other and propagated by the church thru brainwashing by the church elders. If anybody was able to go back in time and get the original story without changes by storytellers, what would you have? In other words, you must read between the lines and make your own conclusion. Just think about the possibility of how things actually could have taken place or what really took place! Now I ask you are the words in the bible and Koran the words of god or the words of man? Please stop and think for yourself. You make the call!

CHAPTER SEVENTEEN

ASTROLOGY

After I finished what I was told to write, knowing that there was something else missing about the subject of religion, I was guided to research more about the subject of religion and the bible. To my amazement, the following is what I found that might change our outlook and belief of religion, *not spirituality or our god.*

First, there is no record of Jesus from childhood until he was about twelve then not until he was about thirty. Second, the scriptures were written from stories passed down, not actual facts at the time they were supposed to take place. It seems to me that everybody that reads the bible and tries to explain and prove what the stories are trying to tell us have not gone far enough into their research. Could this be part of the control that the church has created? The following is what I discovered.

There were many "Gods" with all the same attributes as Jesus prior to the stories of Jesus. The story of the first Jesus, Simon of Persia was the savior before Jesus with Gabriel and Joseph (The first Jesus on Nat Geo on Nov 20, 2009). Then there was Horus in Egypt at about 3000BC, born on Dec. 25, born of a virgin under a star in the east, adorned by 3 Kings, was a teacher at twelve, became a minister at thirty, had twelve disciples, performed miracles, was crucified and was resurrected after three days. Then there was Attis in Greece about 1200BC, born on Dec 25, born of a virgin, performed miracles, was crucified and was resurrected. Then there was Mithra of Persia in 1200BC, born on Dec 25, born of a virgin, was crucified, dead for three days and resurrected. Then Dionysus in Greece at 500BC, born on Dec25, born of a virgin and performed miracles. All of these men had a mother with a first name starting with "M". Now Dec25 is the first day after the winter Solstice, Easter is the Spring Equinox, the Star of Bethlehem is the Star Sirius, the three Kings are the three stars of Orion's belt, the Cross is the Southern Cross or the constellation Crux at the time of the Winter Solstice when the sun is in the middle of the cross. The resurrection is the Spring Equinox when the Sun shines more than fifty percent of the day. Since the earlier people relied on Astrology without all the city lights, to guide and control their lives at this time in history, it is a known fact that all the scriptures were written from stories passed down thru time, and nobody has been able to verify that this information is one hundred percent authentic. These stories from astrology were passed down thru history, and then the people in power used them to create a society of control. The question now is where do we go from here if any of this is an accurate depiction of how we are being controlled? If this astrology information has any credence, then all religions around the world have just lost the basic foundation. Based on this information, could it be that Jesus never actually existed or is Jesus another god carried thru from Pagan times and propagated by the church?

Before you pass judgment and call me a crackpot, go on the internet and look up each of these gods and see what all of the scholars have to say about this subject. Is Jesus a reincarnation of Mithra of Attis? The Vatican was built on the same land as the land that Mithra people did their Worshiping. Since all of the attributes of Jesus are a duplicate of these previous gods, where does that leave us or today's religion?

The main purpose of this book is about control. Could this be a reason that so many people do not believe in god? That these people might know that the religious group is based on false information created by church elders many centuries ago? There are many people that believe in a higher power (god) but not in religion, so now I can say that spirituality is the proper path to reach your god without religion. Religion controls you, but only you control your own spirituality. We are all reaching for freedom from control. I only hope that everybody will take a serious look at how you would like to move forward with your own life. YOU MAKE THE CALL for your own future.

Let's do some research into the last chapter of the bible, Revelation through astrology. Almost every religion around the world has a story about the Apocalypse coming in the year 2012. Most religions specify the year and other religions do not. If we go back to when John wrote these words and follow with the thought that everybody at that time was into astrology very heavily as the Aztec civilization was in their time. We might find that John wrote these things from stories that were passed down thru the ages the same as all the scriptures of the bible. Since very early writings did not exist or have been destroyed thru time, and what has been uncovered about the stories of Jesus, it raises a question about where the stories in Revelation came from. The stories of Satan coming to earth could really be facts from astrology referring to natural earth cycles that will coincide with the Winter Solstice about Dec.21, 2012 that occurs every 25,800 years when all the planets will be in alignment with the center of our Solar System. Reminder, as explained earlier that Satan does not exist in reality, Satan was created by the Church leaders for control. So where do we go from here? Do we believe any of these scriptures as actual fact, or as everything else in the bible, was this another story passed down to keep the populous under control?

I have one more question for everybody. Since there are portraits and busts of many leaders and people that were created at the time that they lived, can you give any explanation as to why there is not one portrait or artifact of what Jesus looked like at the time he was supposed to live? Therefore all of the portraits of Jesus are only mans idea of what we think he should have looked like. So my question to you is this, did Jesus actually live?

SUMMARY

Since all of the stories about Jesus were passed down after the fact and possibly all based on astrology, where does that leave the bible, the Koran and Religion? Could this be the reason that nobody has been able to explain the following? The Star of Bethlehem, who the Three Wise Men were or where they came from, what happened to the Chests of gold and jewels, why Joseph remained a poor man, why there is no record of Jesus as a young boy, why there is no record of Jesus between age twelve and age thirty. Can you explain any of these questions or does the church have all of us so brainwashed that you want to ignore them. Could it be possible that religion is based strictly on astrology from the past? YOU MAKE THE CALL.!!!

CONCLUSION

Being a spiritualist is a faith, not a religion. I use the word church loosely in the following, due to being able to explain and understand. A church is a gathering of three or more people, not a building. Of all the spiritualist churches I have attended, they are simple and unadorned. In simple words, just a roof over your head, to be out of the weather for peace and tranquility, nothing fancy. Some have an altar and fancy candles. These things make us feel at home due to the brainwashing, that we are having a hard time undoing. But it makes us feel good to open up to be more receptive to the power of the universe and our god. This also goes with the music and singing in the church. It makes us feel good and allow us to relax. The more we are relaxed, the easier it is for us to receive the word and message from god. Before going on, please remember who your god is. Your god is your ancestors and guides combined with your spirit.

I have not been in a spiritualist church that passes the plate asking for ten percent of my earnings. All they ever want is enough money to pay for things such as property taxes, electricity, and etc. Due to all the brainwashing, some still use the bible and follow the guidelines of the organized religion (crime). In a spiritual church, you will experience many different things from organized religion. Everybody has a special ability from god, such as Healing, Aura readings, and many more, but few people recognize their own talent. When you go to a spiritualist church, you will see aura readings, healing (laying on of hands), spiritual readings and etc. you might experience the power and energy not felt elsewhere. These things are not Voodoo or Witchcraft. They are the powers of the universe to help and guide us.

The spiritualist faith comes from within you. You do not have to run to a Priest for any answers or to be forgiven for your sins. It can truly only come from within you, from your god, spirits or your soul. You do not need Rosary beads or anything else to remember to guide our thoughts about spirituality. If you are able to slow down and relax enough, to hear and feel your god and guides helping you through life, only then can you start to be a free person shedding some of the controls that organized religion and the state has put on us.

It appears to me that all religions started prior to the time when the Pharaohs were in power, when the church and state were one power. Then religion followed these rules and guidelines. As I said earlier, we the people are so brainwashed from that far back, that it will take many, many years to overcome the brainwashing. But we must start, somewhere, sometime, somehow. The human race must stop acting like animals, fighting and killing each other. The sad part is, as far back as the history records go, this has been the lifestyle of the human race, reaching for world power, reaching for religious power. This has got to stop so humanity can get on one track together for the betterment of all people. If the human race wants to go to space, things will have to change on earth. When countries stop fighting over religion and land, and become really civilized, as we profess to be, and have not yet accomplished. Then the human race will be able to become a universe power, not just a world power. The power and energy of the universe is out there. All we need to do is get all the people on this planet to get together, and combine our resources and technology. Then, with a common faith (spirituality) and goals for humanity, we can advance our combined races for the betterment of mankind. If you follow any of the programs on the Discovery channel or History channel, you will see that the archaeologists and investigators are learning what our ancestors did and how they lived. But, much of the information they are learning, and passing on to us, is guess work. This is the same as Bigfoot, called many different names around the world. They have been seen, tracks found, evidence found, but our scientists do not acknowledge their existence, since there is no hard proof (a body) so far. There have been stories of giant squid for centuries, nobody believed the stories, until, in recent years, when scientists finally got their hard proof.

If you think this book is only one man's opinion, let me explain. The world has watched movies and programs labeled as science fiction. Programs like **Star Wars**, **Star Trek**, to open your minds just a little bit. Do you think that all of these writers, that put these programs together have had the same contact with their guides and spirits (whether they realize it or not), to give us a forewarning and a look into the future of what is coming? What is happening out there right now, that we are not a part of yet? Could this be why there are so many spaceships seen all around the globe? I could elaborate much more on this subject about my personal experience with UFOs, but that is not the intention of my message. The major message is control. We as a human race are not free. This control has been going on for so long, that it must be put in check. The USA was founded on freedom; the country was formed with the motto "One Nation Under God". The problem is that the controlling fathers at that time, being brainwashed by the church, did not realize how much control the church had on the new government, that the State included control of the church. We the people need to reinforce that idea. This country is "One Nation Under God" not under the church. I believe that our courts have gone way too far, and have forgotten what this country is all about. When the minority that complaints about god in the state or schools, they are not really complaining about god, they are complaining about the church. We will always have our god and Jesus to guide us and protect us. We do not need the church as it is today. We need a single spiritual faith, or belief that will be universal around the world. There have been too many wars fought around the globe over religion. We all start out the same, and end up the same. Now let's get what is in the middle the same for everybody, one faith, and one belief for everybody. Stop fighting; love thy neighbor, one faith or belief for all of mankind.

If you go back and study the bible, you will find that today's "Religion" is not what God and Jesus intended. The church leaders could not let go of the old ways when the bible was being compiled, therefore, the old testament was included as part of the bible, and the methods of control were included in the "NEW" Bible for the control by the church. As I said earlier, you must read between the lines, and come to your own conclusion. I would like everybody to understand what religion is really about. That religion is really nothing more than Big Business and Organized Crime. This does not include spirituality or god, because Spirituality is each person answering to their own god without the control by man (leaders in control).

Since it appears that the Catholic church was the original Christian religion and is still following the ways of the Pharaohs and rulers of that time and all other Christian religions are a spin off of the original by mans idea, not god's, I believe this is why we are in this confused state today.

Now when we take a serious look into astrology, this brings up a whole new area of consideration of what the church has been teaching. Can you explain how there have been many men with all the same attributes as Jesus in astrology? We must all take a new look into what the church is trying to cram down our throats as the truth to keep us under their control. I know that there will be many people that are so brainwashed, that they will never consider anything other than what the church leaders have been teaching. This is the same as the archeologist's are learning more and more about past alien contact with the people on our earth. We must all have an open mind to what is or was possible.

COULD SPIRITUALITY BE THE BEGINNING TO A UNIVERSAL FAITH? TO BRING PEACE AND HARMONY TO OUR WORLD??? Could this create a new world order, not financial, but a spiritual bonding around the world?

Looking into the records of astrology, could the church and religion have been built on one lie after another for control? If these astrology records are accurate, where does that leave all the religions of the world? As best as I can understand what has been uncovered, this leaves the religious world as one monstrous lie for many, many years to control the people into submission by the church leaders. Also, could this explain why the Jewish faith does not believe or acknowledge Jesus Christ? Since the Jewish faith was in effect before Christianity was established, what do they know that we have been brain-washed into believing? Since there is no hard proof as to actual fact of what the church has been professing and teaching, where does that leave the church and religion? Now I have a question that should be answered. If the Bible and Koran are very similar, with many of the same stories in them, was the Koran written based on stories passed down also? The Muslim Iman should take a good look into this scenario and see if he can give a better explanation that would make logical sense?

If this information has any credence, then almost every religion in the world should take a good hard look into what the basis of their religion has been formed from. Since the Romans assembled the first bible in about the third century after the fact, where does that leave the general public in regards to what the church has been preaching? This also leaves all of those people that are trying to explain and prove that the writings in the bible are correct or accurate information, in a quandary trying to discover and prove something that never existed.

As stated earlier, when a story is passed around it gets changed as to what each person understands what they think they heard and then gets picked up as fact to be put down in a book. This then allows the powers in charge to enforce what they believe is actual fact. Back when the church was getting started the people in charge had such a hold over the people that their control was considered to be law. This control was a continuation of what the Romans had with all of their god's in the past. Let's see if we can get rid of this antiquated and out of date control. It's about time that YOU MAKE THE CALL.

BOOK TWO

The State

INTRODUCTION

Since I live in the USA, much of book two is directed to situations in this country. If you live in any other country, once we get the church out of the state, you will have to look at the controls that your country has on the people of each and every country. Each and every country has their own laws to control their people that will have to be looked at, and abolished so that everybody can be free as we were intended to be by god.

We the people do not need a small group of people to control our lives as they have been doing for many centuries.

As an example of control by a government, the Vatican has security guards protecting their property, the Swiss Army. How can the Swiss people have a free choice when their government is dedicated to the Catholic church? In this country I call this sideways brainwashing or hidden control.

CHAPTER ONE

CREATION OF STATE

When I say the state, it means any and all forms of government at any level.

The state was created many centuries ago to control the masses in a small area (confined—a city). The powers to be soon realized this was very profitable. So very slowly they kept increasing the amount of control that filled their pockets. When they got too greedy, there was an uprising. But with the army to protect their money, it also protected the unrealistic laws. Soon man became so accustomed to the laws, they became acceptable. Now the state has all the power it needs. Also convincing man that the church was no longer part of the state, this made it much easier for each faction to put controls on the populace without anybody questioning their authority. So for centuries man has been brainwashed from the time of birth to join in with the masses. If anybody challenges the normal procedure, they are either imprisoned for treachery or classified insane. Now the church and state have enough control, that if you don't agree, they will get rid of you by unknown or hidden methods.

The state should be a body of government that controls streets, sewers, water, electricity and etc. The state should never be involved in peoples emotional or religious status. Please take a good look at every government around the world and you will see that every one has this religious faction as part the government function, not spirituality, only control for you and me.

CHAPTER TWO

STATE AND CHURCH

Many countries today still have the church as part of the state. In these countries, from all appearances, the church is the controlling power. Anytime these churches think that they're belief is stronger or better than their neighbors, the state goes to war over religion.

In other countries, where in all appearances, the church is not part of the state, these people will find other reasons to start a war, such as over religious boundaries, or I don't like the way you look, or you might make fun of our people in a cartoon. Most cultures have a religious sect that is so far off base, that any comment or gesture will set off a feud. When this feud gets a big enough, the state steps in to resolve the situation and starts a war. This is very similar to a soccer game. Why is this sport such a national pride as to cause riots and wars?

What I am trying to point out is very clear and simple. If the state was not a part of the church, there would not be wars fought over religion. Refresher comment, religion is nothing more than a following of the masses. The largest proof of this is the state controls the church by means of all the laws they have imposed on the church. No organized church may conduct business until they have satisfied all the laws of the state, then they can call themselves a nonprofit organization. Nonprofit to these groups in many cases is nothing more than a big joke. For the money taken in and the amount of community service performed does not equate to nonprofit. How can nonprofit organization own property and business that produce a profit?

CHAPTER THREE

STUPID LAWS

If we as a whole, would get more involved in our government, and eliminate all the laws of a personal nature. We need to go through the books and get rid of any law that is of a personal nature, not of property or service nature. The only laws that will be then left are those of a property or community service, not directed to help people. Only when this could take place, will the state be free of the church.

Man is not stupid. If and when all (or many) of these controls are removed, things will start to run smoothly on their own. Then the only control by the state needs to have over man is when he directly violates the masses by killing or stealing etc.

The laws of today actually control so much of what man does, that each individual does not really know what freedom is.

If you take a good look at how our society is being controlled by the national and local governments, you will see that the laws that are being passed by the government are getting very close to a Socialist or Communist state. We as the general public must get more involved in the laws that our government is allowed to be put into effect. As an example, go to any government website and look at Bill # HR45 and #HR2159. These bills say anybody that owns a Gun, must register it. If they don't, they are in violation, and subject to a major fine and/or imprisonment. This law is in direct contradiction of the Second amendment of the constitution of the USA. Many country's that have banned guns, have had a major rise in their crime rate with guns and violence has also risen. If we don't do something now this is what to expect. Go to HTTP:// www.Rense.com/general86 /loss.htm on the computer and see what is coming if we get national gun control.

Now please, keep in mind we are talking about control. Let's go into welfare, first the state collects taxes, to create the welfare System to help the needy and deserving people only as a temporary measure. Now the problem is that the state cannot control their own system. Therefore, many people can figure out how to beat the system. There are people on welfare that get their housing paid, and receive more income from the state than the average working person makes. The state is getting too big when they can not control their own control. The message of this is it is a sad state of affairs when the controller is out of control. And this is only one example of all the do-gooder programs that is in shambles. The only department of the state that has complete control is the ones that collect your money.

What I'm asking people, is, where has your drive gone? Back a couple hundred years, there was a major drive to form a new country. This drive was to stop oppression from the government and church. What I see happening today, is as a people, we have let go of any drive or initiative to better ourselves. We sit back and let the state and court system take more and more control of our lives. Why have we become so complacent? This country was founded on "In God We Trust". since this is and was the foundation of the United States of America, why do we allow a minute group of people, to take away the foundation of our country? The courts make us remove anything pretaining to god in any public building. They have removed prayer from public schools. Again, the majority would like to see the prayer added back into schools. Since this country was built on "In God We Trust", all it would take is for the few who don't believe, to temporarily remove themselves from the area of prayer or go back to where they came from where they can have freedom in the faith they believe in. Where is your backbone people? When are you going to say enough is enough? It takes the state a little time to fully take over what matters to us. What we need to do is remove the appointment of Judges from the government control and make them elected officials so the people have more control of the court system. No Judge should be allowed to go against the Constitution and foundation of the USA which says in god we trust. Therefore, all of the laws banning god in public places are technically illegal. What is it going to take for the President to correct this problem? This country was founded on the belief in god, let's keep it that way. A poll was taken recently, about eighty-six percent of the people still wanted god in schools and public buildings. We the people must get our control back. We have already lost too much control to our government by just sitting back and doing nothing. It's time to Change this lazy attitude.

Our children are being brainwashed at such an early age that it is hard to separate their teaching from reality. Now the state has stepped in, in recent years with a department called "Child and Family Services". I have seen the power and control they have. It is unreal, when a child's discipline is taken away from the parents. This is an out of control state. We are not a dictatorship. From what I've seen and experienced, the state should not be able to take an out of control child, without due process of law first. I believe there would not be near as many children causing problems if the parents were allowed to discipline as they use to do many years ago. You would not have children marrying and/or bearing a child. We as adults have to take back control of our lives and get mankind back on track as originally designed. Is this the beginning of a "big brother" society? Why is it illegal to discipline a child in an effort to teach them right from wrong? If the child tells any authority figure that he or she was abused, true or not, that the parent is subject to arrest. This now has created a society that is afraid to do what should be done, and is necessary to bring their own child up in an educated manner. "Child and family services" needs to be done away with and allow the courts only, with documented proof of abuse to handle the situation.

This also brings up the subject of spousal abuse. If in a dispute, one spouse slaps the other party, somebody will go to jail. The state has gone a little too far. Granted, there is a need for some control in this area, but let's keep it in reality and stop wasting money on trivial things. Every time the state gets involved in any disciplinary subject or action, we as the general public, allow the state to go overboard in whatever action is taken. Let's get more involved in control or non control of our lives! If parents were allowed to raise their children with more respect and discipline, like it used to be, maybe we would not have as many difficult children growing up today. We created this situation right after World War ll. I can remember very clearly, after World War II, men coming home from the war saying, my father used to spank me when I was growing up, and I don't want my children to have to go through this. So look at what we created. A society without discipline, therefore a society without respect, and now, giving away our own control. Let's get it together and start getting our own control back. Or would you like to be like England, big brother control. There are 4.3 Million cameras on their city streets, or approximately one camera per every fifteen people. Is this what us Americans want? If we could get the church out of the state, the war, going on for many years between England and Ireland would not exist. This bloodshed between England and Ireland over religion is such a waste. Because the government and church have that much control, how stupid! If the countries over there were not fighting over religion, causing uneasiness between the countries, England would not need as many cameras.

Now we are still talking about control, or loss of control. As I said earlier, the state in an effort to "DO GOOD", created a department called welfare. This was a great idea. The problem here is when welfare was created, there were not enough stop gap measures included in the original guidelines. It did not take long for the lazy, non motivated people to figure out how to cheat the system. This system was intended to help people in need, if there was a medical problem or as temporary unemployment Insurance, not a permanent life style. Taking a good serious look at the welfare system today, first, these people get free rent, free food, all medical services, and cash to boot. It's a very sad situation when these lazy people collect more from the state for doing nothing then many people get from working hard eight to ten hours a day, If these lazy people know the system, they can collect up to $40,000 a year, or even more. In the majority of cases this is more money than people who worked all their lives receive on SSI. This system needs a major overhaul. With the computers we have to verify only one claim per person. Not more than one claim nationwide. Then verify the number of children is accurate and legitimate. Today, first there needs to be a major database for all welfare. Welfare services next needs a time limit, not indefinite. No welfare recipient should receive more money and services than someone that has worked for forty or fifty years, and on SSI. Why are we, as the general public, paying taxes to support someone that is too lazy to go to work? Let's get control of where our tax money goes! As we are told, that SSI is going to go broke in the near future, let's correct welfare and put that money into the SSI fund where it belongs.

Something I feel should be looked into is SSI was created for retired people. Why are many disabled people on SSI and not on welfare? I agree that a disabled person should receive help, but shouldn't they be on welfare or workman's comp instead of SSI in many cases? If our government leaders stopped taking the easy way out and did their job as they should, maybe the SSI system would not be in trouble.

Why are all of our government officials exempt from SSI and medicare? They are all just citizens the same as the rest of us. Why do they deserve special treatment?

Speaking of the SSI system, why was the government ever allowed to borrow so much money from SSI without authorization and never pay it back? This is the major reason that SSI is in trouble.

CHAPTER FOUR

THE PRESIDENT

Let's now go to the top of the government system. Does the president, Congress, or Senate have the general public as first priority? Do you really think the President of this country is going to spend over $50 million on a campaign to receive a salary of about $400,000.00? If you believe this, then you better go back to kindergarten. Take a look at the Kennedy family. Where did this family get their money, legal or illegal? Joe Kennedy was a bootlegger during the prohibition, and the Onasis shipping lines were involved. After the death of J. F. K., who did Jackie Kennedy marry?

And next, the Bush family has always been in oil, for many years. Since this is the case and the Bush family was in control, just look at what happened to the oil prices. Do you really believe that the oil prices were controlled by overseas countries? There is no way to trace the flow of money from the oil producing countries, but, my information (and no way to prove) is that when President Bush went over to the oil producing countries, the secret service men had a hard time carrying all the gifts he received, back to the U.S. Stop and look at what happened to oil prices when the Bush family left office. Just look at the facts, and then read between the lines. You come to your own conclusion.

Did I hear you say that our government is in complete control of our country? That our Commander In Chief controls are military? Then something that I personally experienced should be known. Many of the world banker's are located in Miami Florida. There's an island just south of Miami with an exclusive club. This club is called O.R.C.—Ocean Reef Club. The dues are round $50,000 I was told. In order to own property in this club you must be a multimillionaire, such as the world bankers in Miami. These are the people that control the world politics. Anyway, in the late eighties, the Coast Guard wanted to sink a ship to create an artificial reef on the Atlantic side of southern Florida. But before our Coast Guard could take this ship around the island, they had to wait three weeks so that O. R. C. could move many of their security measures and cameras before our coast guard could take the ship past their Island. Now who is in control?

Let's take a look at today, Mr. Obama during his campaign was going to stop the war in Iraq, Iran and close down Guantanamo as well as other promises. What happened? The President does not have as much power as the politicians would have us believe. To the best of information that I have been able to get so far is that there are approximately 24 levels of National Security and the President is at level 12. This limits his control and also when there is a situation he can deny any knowledge and be honest. All you have to do is look at Area 51. It has been denied by our Presidents, but we see pictures of it all the time. Can anyone tell me why or what is going on with our national security when our President is denied information about what is going on? Even the President is controlled.

On the HINT channel aired on Dec 1,2010 see "Presidents Book of Secrets" to get a better idea of what is not known about our Government system.

CHAPTER FIVE

GOVERNING BODIES

If the Senate and Congress were there for the public interest, don't you think they would be there on the job every day like any other job? How come the majority of the time, both houses are missing many of their constituents? They claim to be doing their work, but when both houses are in session, all our elected officials are supposed to be there. Where are they and what are are they doing? Could it be that these elected officials are out with special interest groups instead of doing their job? Both houses have recess time to do outside work, but there seems to be a lack of interest in the job they were elected to do. It appears to me, that we the public have lost control of the people we elected to speak for us. If these politicians were on any other job, they would be fired for not going to work. These politicians have the ability not to go to work and then give themselves a raise. How come at the same time they give themselves a raise, why did they stop any increase to everybody that is on SSI? This sure looks like another out of control system. Why, when the Politicians go on a business trip, does the whole family go with them? We the people must fly Coach, but they fly First Class. Please take a good look at this system on a National and a State level. I believe, that we the public, should demand that their salaries be reduced until these politicians start doing their job and reporting to work every day as hired (elected) to do. If these people were on the job more often, maybe there would not be as many stupid laws passed. It would be much harder for special Interest groups to get laws in their favor passed. Even though there are laws in place to stop payola from taking place, do you really believe it does not still exist? There are so many ways to get around this situation. This is why so many people want to be a politician, for personal gain. If you go back in the early 1900's, this is how the Federal Reserve was created, there were only **three** members in session when it got passed.

Another point of interest is the Congress and Senate does not pay into Social Security. They receive their salary for life after leaving their job. If this was to be changed, where they were now in the Social Security system, don't you think that they would have more interest in how retired people were to receive an income after retirement and also hospitalization? This also applies to all government workers. Why do the government employees all have a different retirement program than the rest of the population? Shouldn't they have the same conditions as the rest of the population? This system has been in effect for so long that it will take a major effort for the population of this Country to get this changed. We need to get this on the Ballot for the public to vote on in order to get it changed.

Now to the Senate and Congress at the federal and state levels. It took the press to break this true story about the tobacco industry, for this industry that had been paying enormous amounts of money to keep their industry making enormous profits in hiding the truth from the general public. The point of this is still going on with the alcohol Industry. You've seen taxes being raised on everything except alcohol. To give you an example, Phoenix Arizona recently added a $1.00 tax to everyone in the city that receives a water bill to cover the cost of all the people going to jail for drunk driving. This to me seems so ridiculous. If we have a problem with alcohol and the general public that uses this substance, then why do we tax something else to cover the cost? What is wrong with our lawmakers? Why has there never been a tax put on alcohol to pay for drunk drivers? When are they going to do the job that they were elected to do? This is a national problem, not a single local problem. If Phoenix Arizona gets the money from water users, for drunk drivers, then where does this rest of the country get the money to cover the cost of drunk drivers?

Next out of control, the prison system in America is mainly big business. America has the largest per capita inmates of any country in the world. The majority of inmates in our prisons should not be there. Our "Do Good" society again has gone out of control. This is mainly due to the Hearst publishing company many years ago. Many years ago, Mr. Hurst wanted to sell more newspapers. That's when he contrived a ridiculous story about cannabis. Hurst wrote and produced movies about how cannabis led to suicide, rape, murder and more. All of his stories were unfounded and untrue. On the HINT channel see "Marijuana a Cronic History" aired on Nov 3, 2010

This is where our government is stupid and ridiculous; it costs the taxpayers up to $300.00 a day to incarcerate each person, major waste of money (that's our government). If you go to Europe, in some countries; cannabis is sold openly on the streets. Many of those countries do not even incarcerate their people for the use of cannabis, only the sale. We are running out of prison space. That means more wasted money to build more prisons. Now on the other hand, if cannabis was made legal, it could be taxed the same as cigarettes. Now our government could save the money going to the big business, the prison system, and collect the same amount from the sale of cannabis. If cannabis was made legal, do you think it would be as popular as it is? Police could continue to arrest people for DUI as they do now, not for just possession of Cannabis. California is going to have the legalization of marijuana on the ballot in 2010. If this bill passes, it will reduce the number of inmates in the prisons and take a major punch out of the Cartels control. This will also help to reduce the killings around the world by these people.

Next, many people get travel papers to come to the USA. They live here for many years; they cannot be bothered to become a citizen of the USA. They then get into a legal situation and a judge will sentence them to time in jail or prison. These people spend time in our prison system, complete their sentence, and then the I. N. S. steps in and proceeds to deport these people and take away their papers. We support these people for months or Years and then throw them out of the country? Can you tell me why, when they are sentenced, instead of wasting taxpayers' money on supporting people that are leaving the country anyway. Why doesn't I. N. S. step in at that time and deport them before we support these offenders? This should be done to all non serious offenders. Big business, the prisons would lose a lot of money and maybe even lower our taxes. But to me, the wrong people are in control of our money (taxes).

Now, talking about taxes, another out of control situation, why do our leaders let other countries control our money? As an example, the import duty on U.S. products versus their Import duty on our products. Japan, the last I heard had an extremely high import duty on our motorcycles going into their country, but we have a small duty on their motorcycles coming into the USA. Also we allow other countries to ship into us, parts at a very low Import duty, knowing that all these Parts will be assembled here to sell their products at a lower price. Why do our leaders continually sell the U.S. short? If a country has an import duty for our products, then our duty should be equal to theirs. If we know parts are going to be assembled here, then they should be taxed the same as a complete item. If the import and export duty was equal going both ways, don't you think that we might keep more jobs right here in USA?

Now, let's talk about control, hidden control. For the past fifty or sixty years, there has been a lack of interest by our government to support our country. There has been a major drive to promote foreign trade. Bring in foreign products that are in many situations, of a lesser quality, sometimes at a lower price? So in bringing in foreign products, we are sending our jobs out of our country. Just take a look at some of our major brands, made in some other country. Do any of you ever look at where these products are made? I recently went to a national discount store, and inspected the labels on a product I wanted to buy, only to discover that the national brand was made in some other country and the USA brand (not popular) was lower in price and just the same quality. Why are we allowing so many products to be imported? Why are we buying so many imported products? This to me is the hidden control by our government. If we want to end up as a work force like China or Japan, then buy as many imported products as possible. All of you auto workers that are out of a job, that are driving a foreign car, what do you expect to happen to your job when you cannot support your own country? This also includes all of you people driving foreign autos. Example—KIA started 15 years ago with only one model, and today they have 11 models. Are these your Jobs in Korea? If you think that buying their products is helping those people, then just look at their living conditions, it has not improved anything. We Americans have gotten too greedy. I used to live in Cleveland, Ohio, and watched one company after another leave that city. The unions and workers continually wanted more money and less responsibility. Therefore, manufacturing and other companies had to move someplace else, in order to compete in the market place. And now you have the nerve to ask why am I losing my job? We as the blue collar worker have gotten too complacent and greedy. That is why so many jobs have left our country. It might cost a little more on some products, but it might save some USA jobs, or even bring some jobs back to our country. If you don't think that this is hidden control, then why is our government still pushing for more foreign trade? At the rate we are going right now, our economy will be no better than those foreign countries we are supporting. We cannot continue to ask for more wages and working conditions if we want to maintain our job market in this country. In many situations the Unions have gone too far for the working man. We the people have to be realistic in our request, to stop the foreign trade at the level it is at and start bringing production back to our country. As I said earlier, our government officials do not have the general public as their main interest. They have been selling our country short very slowly. If you think my statements are inaccurate, study the progress of what has been going on very slowly, for many years. One company after another moving overseas, or just buying their products from other countries and putting their name on them, just for profit of their company, with no regard of the consequences except profit.

An example of hidden control, Walmart, the world's largest retailer, a USA company, supports our community's and our Troops. Target is a French company, Does Not Support our troops. Why do we support a company that does not support our Country?

I call this hidden control by our government. Also, Levi Strauss had advertised San Francisco, but they are no longer made in the USA. Levi never lowered their prices when they went outside of our country. Next, the USA owes China many billions dollars. China does not want this amount to be paid because it would raise their economy. Therefore, they would have to raise their prices and lose the jobs over there. Isn't this control by both Governments?

Something the average American is not aware of, there is a group called Infraguard that reports to the F.B.I.. Infraguard is just your general public. They keep track of citizens and report to the FBI anything out of the ordinary. This sounds to me like the NATZI control. This appears like Big Brother control going into effect.

Now there is the Global Warming Scare. Yes we must get a better control on our destruction of the planet, but the government is going overboard. The money being generated by this scare is totally out of control. The government official's that are promoting this are getting very rich from of this program. Also could this be the beginning of a World Control Government. This will be similar to Europe going to a common currency, to get everybody under a common Government, worldwide. Or could Global Warming just be a natural process of the Earth as in the past?

Something that every American should be aware of is the following chapter.

CHAPTER SIX

NEW WORLD ORDER

Now that we are talking about Control, I would like to expose you to a possible unknown faction that has been working for many years. There is a group that is trying to get control of the world. Their main purpose is to eventually have a one world government, one monetary system, one universal language, and population control. It is called the Bilderberg group, consisting of 120 members from around the world. Every President of the USA has attended these meetings for more than the last thirty plus years and heads of the media (TV and print). This group meets once a year to decide on the next action of control. Each decision is to slowly take control of each and every faction on the Earth. One of the visible things that have been done is the EURO monetary system. Some of the hidden items are artificial sweeteners. Nutrasweet contains Aspertame which is a strong poison, originally developed as a poison for animals which did not work effectively; instead it is given to the population. Splenda contains Sucralose which has more in common with DDT than food. Since the Food and Drug Administration originally found the items unhealthy, how did they get approved for public consumption? I believe these and many other artificial food additives are getting approved as a method to reduce the population of the world. In California the waste water from treatment plants is used to water the crops. This water is deemed as good, but how come there are so many vegetables scares from California crops? Do you realize that the drugs (medicine) being flushed into our waste water are not filtered out before it is recycled into our drinking water? It might be a small amount, but how safe is this water for us to drink?

The flooding of USA with foreign products has been part of their plan for control. By doing this they can get the economy of many countries on an equal level. This then would give these people more control world wide. This group would like to see the population reduced to make it easier to control. There is a structure in Georgia, USA called the Georgia Guide Stone or Georgia Stonehenge that explains what their main objective is, reduce the population of the world to only 500,000,000. The Georgia guide stone is written in eight language's. It is not known who had this structure erected. These people have enough money, but want to Control the world. By reducing the population they can maintain control of the populous a lot easier.

These people are trying to create a system that we do not want to see go into effect. They want to create the North American Union which would include the USA, Canada and Mexico as ONE country. Also the South America Union which would include all of South America as one country, the Europe Union, Africa Union and Asia Union. Each of these would be a state with only one Army for the World.

For more information on the New World Order, look it up on your computer and go to the Rothchild Illuminate to understand what is being planned.

CHAPTER SEVEN

CONSPIRACY THEORY

Let's go to the destruction of the World Trade Center of 9/11. I believe this destruction was orchestrated by the Bilderberg Group with the help of our government. The metal structure was painted with an explosive paint, a mixture of paint and "Super Thermite". This material in a liquid state is not harmful, but once dried, it becomes highly explosive, burning above 2500 deg. After this disaster, a maintenance worker explained this situation. About six to eight seconds before the airplane hit the tower there was a major explosion in the basement of tower. Many people that were there at that time reported that there was an explosion in the basement at the same time as the airplane hit the towers. The fuel from the plane does not burn hot enough to melt steel but the paint that was used does get hot enough to melt steel. There was residue of Super Thermite found in the dust after the destruction of the towers. Could this also explain what happened to building #7 which was never explained in the official 9/11 report? This was a controlled explosion to blame the terrorist so they could continue the WAR. In the official 9/11 report, it states that the flight recorders were not found, but rescue workers reported that they had seen flight recorders being removed from the area, four of them. Why was all the steel removed and melted as fast as possible before any testing could be done to determine what took place? Something else that is of interest seems very strange that the military was on a training mission at that time and were told to stand down. In military terms this is called a false front. It was also reported that the terrorists were in the cockpit of the planes when they left the airport. There are too many items of interest not included in the official 9/11 report. Such as what happened to building #7? How could this building get demolished when no airplane hit it? The report never mentioned anything about the explosions in the basement's of the twin towers which was reported by many people. The 9/11 report said that a plane hit the Pentagon, but there was no Plane or Plane parts found at or around the Pentagon. We have had no explanation how this situation existed. Please remember while reading this we are talking about Control!

The war is a money making proposition. It is a known fact that of most wars, the world bankers are funding both sides for financial gain. To emphasize this fact, do you realize that the U.S.A. Federal Reserve Bank is not owned or controlled by the USA Government; it is owned and controlled by the World Bankers. This is why the USA government has to pay interest to the Federal Reserve Bank, why would you charge yourself interest? At the rate our government is borrowing from the Federal Reserve Bank, the government will only be able to pay the interest therefore never getting out of debt which will only continue to raise inflation. The more the USA borrows from the world bank, the more they can control our government. I believe the interest should only be to private industry, NOT to our own government. In other words, the world bankers control all the financial institutions in the world which the Bilderberg Group is part of. The Federal Reserve and world bankers are able to create paper money without any collateral to backup what they have created. Therefore when the US borrows money from the Federal Reserve, we are paying interest on money that never actually existed. This money only shows up on paper, the same as the National Debt. How is that for control? Hidden control. How many of the public do understand what is going on?

Something I have been aware of for a long time but could not get enough information on until recently. Shortly after WWII there was a meeting between Chang Chi Shek, Stalin, Churchill and Roosevelt that there would not be any more wars fought in First World Countries, only in Third World Countries where no directive could be achieved. If you stop and take a serious look at all the Wars since WWII, there has not been a resolution from any of the Wars. Since the rest of my information is copyrighted and I cannot print it, please get a copy of the following books—American Conspiracies by Jesse Ventura—The Secret Team and J.F.K. by Col Fletcher Prouty where he explains about the Black Opps and The Secret Team. Also look up on the computer "Ownership of Federal Reserve".

If you believe this is only one person's opinion, look at what other people in the world ideas are, on the internet look up www.prisonplanet. com, www.prisonplanet.com/-endgame, www.zeitgeistmalovie.com and www.infowars.com. On the TruTV channel, lookup "Conspiracy Theory" by Jesse Ventura, there is more than one program that might explain what is going on in our world.

Since WWII sports have gotten extremely popular. Could this be part of their plan so most people will not pay attention to what World Bankers and Politics are doing to our freedom? Take a closer look at what they are doing to our lives and you make the call.

Another subject that the average person is not aware of. There is a Military program called HAARP that has been around for a long time. This program was originally started as a national defense project. Since it's inception the government has learned that there are many more areas of interest that they can use. The most important one to us is where they can control the weather. This area of interest to the government has been around since about 1958. Of all the interesting articles I have read, most of them are directed at the Alaska installation, but investigation discovered there are many more around the world. There is an insulation in Norway, Russia, China, Peru, Puerto Rico, Europe and the Ukraine. All you need to do is look at what has happened to the weather in the last few years. What are the governments around the world doing to us? There are over 400,000 articles on the internet about HAARP. For more info lookup

WWW.cyberspaceorbit.com/phikent/haarp/weather.html.

One more item of interest is the USA government has a "Black Budget". This is a subject that many people do not pay attention to.

Are you aware that of the average annual US budget includes about Fifty billion dollars and much of money has a simple title with no accountability or record of where this money goes or without any tractability. There is also a secret black budget that the congress has no knowledge, information or control of. Why is the US government keeping so much information a secret form the public? They say it is a subject of National Security. I believe they have gone overboard on the subject of national security in a method of control. Is this what we as the national public want from our government? We as the public must get more involved in what our government body is doing to us. Is this control what we want or are we going to take much longer? You make the call! Lets get more involved into what is happening to our lives!

CHAPTER EIGHT

FREEDOM OF SPEECH AND PRESS

In recent years there have been too many occasions where the media has turned their cheek at informative information necessary for the general public.

Just look at the Fox Network, they got into trouble with the Government for certain programs they had on the air. Then, what about all the Tea Parties that never got covered by the press, especially the one in Nevada? Why are so many things on You-Tube removed by the government, things that have nothing to do with national security, just general information or what is controlling our lives? Are our government leaders forgetting about the Constitution? This goes along with all the laws that are being passed that the press is afraid of or being told not to print or put on the air. When after a time a subject appears in print that no longer matters and you ask why didn't we hear about this at that time? Control!

There have been many national reporters over many years that seem to just disappear without any reason or explanation as to why they lost their job, especially after giving their personal opinion. When you read the newspaper or watch T.V. and then later on find out that there was a news item that never got reported, how does that make you feel? Did you ever give it any thought as to why?

CONCLUSION

I could elaborate into much more detail on the government and their control, but it would be redundant. I am only trying to lay some ground work for the general public to look at what is taking place and how the system is controlling everybody's life.

The first thing is our President is only a small part of the problem. Our law makers are the major problem, the congress and senate (federal and state) keep passing laws without any concern of the general public. Many of these people have been in office way too long, it seems they have lost sight of their main purpose, too much special interest. Also our judicial system has lost sight of why they are in office. How can a murderer get a shorter prison sentence than someone one with a DUI? Why are so many law enforcement officials afraid of the law makers and the judicial system? Why do hardened criminals have more rights than the average citizen? The ACLU has gone way too far, they need to be abolished. The only Sheriff I know of that does his job to the letter of the Law is Sheriff Joe in Maricopa County, Az. We need more men like this, to protect the people.

First we need to limit law makers to a two term limit, the same as the President. Second we need to abolish their Golden Pension Plan and put them on the Social Security, the same as the average person that pays their wages. We need to be able to remove a Judge that is not doing their job (not enforcing the laws as required) or being too lenient. Maybe this way the law enforcement will do a better job of keeping the general public safe. We need to abolish the Political parties for a common sense government.

Now we need to force the courts to reinstate "In God We Trust" into our lifestyle. We need to bring the laws of the **nation** back to the people, not what special interest groups want. **Lets put the control back to the people of the nation.** When was the last time your senator or congress representative **asked your opinion** before they passed a bill? This used to be an unwritten requirement of their office, but they seem to have forgotten about the people of the nation, they only think of their self interest. These officials are supposed to be working for us. What happened?

What surprises me the most is that the general public around the world does not seem to care what happens to their future. I sit back and watch the new generation of people waste their time on sports and video games with no concern as to what the government is doing, except to complain about the way their leaders are ruining things that control their lives. Back in the past, our forefathers fought to free themselves from the government control and started a new country. The only problem is they brought many of the controls with them and incorporated these controls into the new government without realizing the future effect it would have on the people. There were not enough safety measures put into the new government to protect the people from future aggression. The only method the people have today, that I can see is a mass uprising to let our politicians know how unhappy the general public is. We must stop the aggression of these leaders and get our country back!!!